Augustine E Costello

History of the Fire and Police Departmetns of Paterson, N.J.

Their Origin, Progress and Development

Augustine E Costello

History of the Fire and Police Departmetns of Paterson, N.J.
Their Origin, Progress and Development

ISBN/EAN: 9783337256609

Printed in Europe, USA, Canada, Australia, Japan

Cover: Foto ©ninafisch / pixelio.de

More available books at **www.hansebooks.com**

HISTORY

OF THE

Fire and Police Departments

OF

PATERSON, N. J.

Their Origin, Progress and Development.

THE OLD AND THE NEW.

OUR TWIN PROTECTORS.—THE VOLUNTEER AND PAID FIRE ORGANIZATIONS.—GALLANT FIRE FIGHTERS. POLICE PROTECTION AND LAW AND ORDER. A WELL DISCIPLINED FORCE.—BIOGRAPHICAL AND HISTORICAL. EFFICIENT FIRE AND POLICE DEPARTMENTS.

ILLUSTRATED.

Sold by Subscription Only.

PATERSON, N. J.:
THE RELIEF ASSOCIATION PUBLISHING CO.
1893.

INTRODUCTORY.

THE compiler has to acknowledge at the outset his indebtedness for much valuable material, which he has used without stint, to a historical *brochure* on the fire department, published two years ago. The facts therein contained are vouched for by ex-Chief McKiernan and Chief Stagg. As the story was tersely and accurately told, it was adopted in the main, without transposition or alteration of any consequence. Other features entirely original have been added, bringing the review of events to date.

The facts contained in the sketch of the police department have been, in great part, obtained at police headquarters through the courtesy of the Commissioners and Chief Graul. The compiler is also indebted to the centennial edition of the Paterson *Evening News* for valuable data. Both departments are well organized and their respective duties are ably administered. Paterson is well served by her police and firemen; that fact is amply demonstrated by the records of the departments, and freely acknowledged by the press and public. There are eighty-six policemen and fifty-eight firemen. Their respective commanders are experienced officers and have the respect of the men and the confidence of the community.

CHAPTER I.

"THE LYONS OF AMERICA."

What a Century Has Done for Paterson—Alexander Hamilton—The "Society for Establishing Useful Manufactures"—The First Cotton Mill—Business Development of the City—The Great Falls.

PATERSON is celebrated as the "Lyons of America," as a compliment to the quantity and quality of its product in manufactured silks.

It is just a century since Paterson was founded as a manufacturing town. The site was selected as affording the most numerous and striking advantages for a manufacturing center. It was the far-seeing mind of Alexander Hamilton that marked out the locality as specially adapted for great industrial activities, and the "Society for Establishing Useful Manufactures" (organized by Alexander Hamilton) laid the foundation of the present city. When the first factory was built, there were about ten houses within the limits of the present city. The society's charter was signed by Governor William Paterson, and it was this that caused the city to be named after him. These are the few and brief foundation facts that have caused a primitive wilderness to develop into a bustling city of 80,000 inhabitants.

When the city of Paterson was incorporated in 1850 it had a population of 11,341. In ten years these figures had expanded to 20,478; in 1865 the city's census was 50,950; 1885, 63,279; and in 1890 the population had reached to 78,358.

The debt of the city is less per capita than that of any city of the state. Jersey City owes $120 per head; Newark, $60; Hoboken, $35; Camden, $28; Paterson, $20.

The original and uppermost idea was, undoubtedly, the manufacture of cotton goods on a large scale, but the production of other necessary domestic articles also was contemplated. It was from the start a city of great expectations, its founders going so far in their extravagant enthusiasm as to believe, as many of them did, that at the location selected by the society all the manufactures of any account in the Union would finally center. The glorious future of the country was then unknown to mortal, and as this was the first organized attempt to establish anything like an industrial center, the success of the undertaking was regarded with the most sanguine expectations. This, indeed, is a historical example of the fact that the founders had builded better than they knew, and, as the result proved, their wildest dreams of success have been more than realized.

Alexander Hamilton, Washington's first secretary of the treasury, as already stated, first conceived the plan or idea of founding the nucleus of the city of Paterson. He had early become convinced that the United States would never be really free and independent of Great Britain until they could manufacture goods enough for their own consumption, and one of his first acts as the head of the treasury department was to endeavor to enlist Congress in support of his views on this subject. The enterprise, we learn from the history of Bergen and Passaic counties, was worked up with great skill and industry until the immense capital of one hundred thousand dollars was subscribed for the projected company; a vast sum to invest in manufactures in those days. The new company was the largest, if not the only one of the kind, in the whole United States.

Hamilton and his associates concluded to locate their works at the Passaic Falls, as affording the finest water-power anywhere within convenient reach of New York or Philadelphia, and then they applied to the New Jersey legislature for an act to incorporate them. The bill became a law on the 22d of November, 1791.

In the year 1837 the County of Passaic was formed from portions of Essex and Bergen, and Paterson became the county seat. In 1838 the population had reached 9,048.

The advisability of changing the form of government from a township to that of a city was fully discussed, resulting, on March 19th, 1851, in the approval by the governor of a bill passed by the Legislature granting a charter to the City of Paterson.

An election was held under the charter on April 14th, 1851, for the filling of municipal offices. The first meeting of the Council was held at City Clerk Socrates Tuttle's office on the south side of Congress street, on Tuesday morning, April 22d, 1851, for the appointment of city officers.

The Great Falls of the Passaic, or "Passaick," as it was called in the early days, has the extraordinary watershed of over 800 square miles. The changes made at and about the falls are almost inconceivable. At first a slender dam was built 200 yards higher up stream than the present one, just above the falls, at La Fontaine's Gap near the bend of the river, the ravine having been converted into a reservoir out of which the current passed into what is now the middle raceway. This water was conveyed 150 yards to the society's first factory off Mill street at the corner of Passaic, as those streets were afterward laid out.

The present dam was constructed in 1838-40, thereby converting the water into an artificial channel constructed across the deep ravine and through the rocks. From this point it is made to turn in succession three tiers of factories, the height of the fall allowing three raceways, the water being used successively that number of times, after which it is once more discharged into the river at a distance of nearly half a mile from the point of leaving it. The minimum supply for mill purposes in a dry season is fifty square feet; the aggregate horse-power is 2,646. The estimate of manufacturers is that a square foot of water is equal to 21 horse-power gross and 19 horse-power net. The society owns rights and franchises for water storage by which it is claimed the present supply would be quadrupled if found necessary. It is estimated that the average annual rental received by the society per square foot is $750. The

HON. THOMAS BEVERIDGE,
MAYOR.

estimate of manufacturers of the average cost of the water is $37.50 per horse-power per annum.

The fact that the important water franchise and a great part of the land on which the city of Paterson is built were held by the society under perpetual charter, with provisions exempting from tax and granting in all respects very sweeping powers, including the right of exercising municipal government over several square miles of territory, has been regarded by some as a very great disadvantage and as having retarded the growth of the city at an earlier date. It was claimed that the high rates demanded on leased water privileges, as for the mill sites owned by it, not only discouraged but in some instances drove away from the place wealthy men and strong corporations who otherwise would gladly have located here. The current method of leasing, for a term of twenty-one years, with a right of purchase was regarded as pernicious in the degree that under this system the society had the power to exact higher rates than were equitable or profitable to purchasers.

These objectionable features, however, are of only antiquarian interest, as such disabilities have long since been removed. The society, in 1848, concluded to sell outright in fee. The result on the prosperity of the young city was most salutary.

Paterson is favored in other ways. The Morris canal runs through the city, and a very large freight business is done upon it, mostly coal and iron for the locomotive works, mills, etc. The Passaic river runs also through the city and is navigable from the Dundee dam to the Broadway bridge. A survey of the river has been made by U. S. engineers, who have pronounced the work of making the river navigable to the heart of the city feasible. The time is not far distant when the river frontage will be in demand for manufacturing purposes and the shores of Dundee lake will be lined with factories, ice houses, lumber yards, oil warehouses, etc.

The Valley of the Rocks is a wild glen where both Washington and Lafayette used to love to wander. The Revolutionary camp ground was near the falls, on the slope of the Totowa hills.

THE COTTON INDUSTRY.—Inspired by Alexander Hamilton, the Society for Establishing Useful Manufactures made preparations for the erection of a cotton mill to be equipped with the novel water-power machines (December 5, 1791). This mill was erected on the west side of the present Mill street, a short distance north of Market street. It was the summer of 1794 before the mill was got into operation. This first New Jersey cotton mill was a small affair. The workmen had to be imported from England, Ireland and Scotland. Owing to poor management the mill did not prove a success, and in March, 1797, it was decided to lease the mill. With its destruction the manufacture of cotton bade fair to cease in Paterson, but the revival of the industry was rapid and remunerative.

In 1810 the production of cotton, linen and woolen cloth for the year amounted to 201,836 yards in families, and 456,250 yards of cotton goods, such as cassimeres, stripes, checks, shirtings, corduroys and fancy goods. There were

585 looms in operation—102 for weaving cotton goods—of which 70 were driven by water-power. Henceforth the business history of Paterson was one of constant development and progression.

CHAPTER II.

SKETCH OF THE OLD FIRE DEPARTMENT.

An Organization that Did Notable Service and Produced a Devoted Body of Men—Their Services Briefly Reviewed—Introduction of the Steam Engine—Some Big Fires.

THE beginnings of the fire department of Paterson were humble, as became the modest little manufacturing village located by Alexander Hamilton at "The Great Falls of the Passaick." Several mill owners had small hand-engines, not much better than a good-sized hand-squirt, and these were used with more or less effect at the occasional fires that awoke the villagers from their quiet, hum-drum life.

The first fire company was organized July 4th, 1815, and was appropriately called after the river that flowed by the settlement and furnished the mills and factories with (at that time) unlimited power. Passaic No 1 was the only company until February, 1821, when Neptune No. 2 was placed on duty, with a new engine built by James Smith, of New York. Other companies followed, and as the village developed into a town and ultimately grew into a city, the department increased in efficiency and usefulness, until it has reached a position that entitles it to praise and distinction amongst the fire fighters of America. Paterson is a leading manufacturing center, containing many tall buildings, the floors of which are saturated with oil, and containing heavy machinery covered with inflammable material in course of manufacture, all of which are capable of making trouble for the firemen, should a fire occur in their immediate vicinity.

Old residents of Paterson say that John Parke brought the first fire engine to this city. Mr. Parke was in business in Market street, near Mill, as early as 1807, spinning cotton and candle wick. In May of that year his mill burned down and the works were removed to Boudinot, now Van Houten street, where Mr. Parke erected a small frame building. In 1810-11 he built a brick and stone mill which now forms a part of the Phœnix silk works. At the close of the war of 1812 Parke failed, and the property passed out of his hands.

Passaic 1 was the only company in the village until December 1820, when a new company known as Neptune 2 was organized, going into service in February, 1821. This year the legislature erected the thickly settled portion of the village into a fire district with power to tax the inhabitants for fire protection. The first meeting of the Paterson Fire Association was held December 2, 1821. It was voted to raise by tax $2,300, and the fire wardens were directed to pay the militia fines of the firemen if they did not exceed $3.00 per man. August 3, 1825, the value of the real and personal property of the Fire Association was $2,325.94. The hook and ladder house was worth $29.25. The debts were $55.94. John Benson was foreman of No. 1 and David Reed of No. 2. In March, 1829, the first lot of sewed hempen hose was purchased. Before that time leather riveted hose had been used. Peter Tice built a house for the truck company at a cost of $150. The residents of Manchester township petitioned the board of wardens for fire protection, but the wardens refused, it being out of the limits of the association. April, 1830, gates were placed on the Dublin Spring brook at Congress street, Ellison street, Van Houten street and Broadway for the purpose of damming the water in case of fire. November, 1830, the Fire Association at their annual meeting instructed the wardens to endeavor to procure the passage of an act exempting firemen from militia and jury duty after serving seven years as firemen. This is believed to be the first firemen's exemption law that was passed in New Jersey.

In December, 1836, the firemen for the first time were given an opportunity to nominate their Chief and Assistant Engineers, John G. Bates for Chief, Nathaniel Lane First Assistant, and Albert I. Hopper Second Assistant being named. The wardens were not pleased with the nominees, and laid the question over, but as the firemen stood firm the wardens receded from their position and the nominations were confirmed. January 23, 1837, the wardens voted "That each engine company be allowed for refreshments when on duty at fire as follows: For one hour $2.50, for two hours $3.50, for four hours $5, and no more to be paid by the treasurer." Old firemen say that it was not at all unusual to run out five times in one night. November 15,

1837, the Chief was voted a salary of $50. In 1840 the firemen were given the privilege of voting directly for Chief and Assistant Engineers. The election was held at Peter Archdeacon's Museum hotel, corner of Smith and Main streets. William Cundell was elected Chief; Titus Ward and Cornelius H. Post Assistant Engineers.

The wardens of the Fire Association governed the department until April, 1855, when they relinquished their charge to the care of the city authorities (Paterson having been made a city in 1851). Until 1854 all the engines in Paterson were of the goose neck style of build except the Phœnix engine, which was a double deck engine. In that year the wardens ordered a piano box engine from Van Ness, of New York, for Engine Company No. 1, but the weight of the engine was against it, and a lighter engine of the same style was purchased for the company from James Smith, of New York.

When the city took charge of affairs improvements were made at once, new houses were built, new apparatus purchased, and in a few years the efficiency of the department was greatly increased. In the first thirty years of the existence of the department the houses were small, one-story frame buildings, 10x20x8 in size. Sometimes they had holes cut in the rear wall to permit the ends of the brakes to protrude. A stationary bench was built around the two sides and rear of the house and furnished the seating accommodations for the members. A stove, a table and a lamp was the usual outfit of an engine house in the primitive days of the department. Latterly the company's quarters were built of brick and were commodious and comfortable, the upper room, or parlor, being furnished in gorgeous style.

January, 1858, the Fire Committee reported to the Board of Aldermen, in response to a request for information, that the amount of pay received by the several fire companies from January, 1856, to January, 1858, was $1,454.61. The committee suggested a fixed amount of pay per annum. This was done and the Board voted to pay first-class engine companies $300.00 per annum; second-class companies $200.00; hook and ladder companies $250.00, and hose companies $200.00. The ordinance fixing the salaries went into effect March 1st, 1858.

Water for fire and domestic use was first introduced into the city in 1855 by the Passaic Water Company. In September, 1856, the city made a contract with the company for one hundred hydrants.

In November, 1857, three two-wheeled jumpers were built for the use of the companies having piano box engines. Previous to this the hose had been carried on reels fastened upon the boxes of the engines.

The volunteer firemen of Paterson, in common with firemen everywhere, bitterly opposed the introduction of steam fire engines. They looked upon it as the death knell of the volunteer system, and hence they regarded it with anything but feelings of satisfaction. The credit of the introduction of steam into the Paterson department belongs to Washington Engine Co., No. 3, and particularly to ex-Chief John McKiernan, ex-Chief Daniel McClory, ex-Asst.-Chief Patrick Chapman, Henry Barclay (now a police

JOHN STAGG,
CHIEF.

JOHN GILMORE,
ASSISTANT CHIEF.

sergeant), and Andrews J. Rogers, all of whom were members of No. 3.

In the fall of 1860, No. 3 visited Albany, Troy and Poughkeepsie. While upon their trip they witnessed several tests of steamers (the Arba Read at Troy and Cataract 4 at Poughkeepsie). Upon their return to Paterson the above-named gentlemen began to agitate the question. It required considerable labor to persuade the company to take any stock in the affair. However, as a result of their efforts the company petitioned the board of aldermen to furnish them with a steam fire engine, offering to pay $1,000 of the cost and reserving the right to buy the city's interest in the machine whenever the company could raise the necessary funds.

The petition was referred to the fire committee, and in a few weeks they reported unfavorably, giving as a reason that "the city was not disposed to enter into a joint stock speculation with a fire company. That steam engines were as yet an experiment and none of the committee had ever seen one of them in operation."

It is an interesting fact that the chairman of the committee was foreman of one of the engine companies. This was intended as a dampener and partly effected its purpose, but McKiernan was not discouraged and found another way to accomplish his object. Ex-Chief Nat Lane, by whom McKiernan was employed, furnished Lee & Larned, of New York, with the brass work for their engines, and he was an enthusiast in everything that pertained to fire apparatus. Messrs. Lane and McKiernan requested Lee &

Darned to send an engine to Paterson on trial. The firm had a small engine named the "Mary Ann." This was brought up, and was received by No. 3. A parade was made through the city, followed by a dinner to which the city authorities and all the prominent citizens were invited. A fireman's dinner without speeches would be an anomaly and this one was no exception to the rule. Foreman McKiernan had his say, of course, and in his remarks he recited the difficulty he had encountered in procuring the presence of the machine; told of the offer the company had made to the city and closed by saying that if the city would not buy improved apparatus the firemen would procure it without their aid, and said that the company stood ready to pay $1,000 toward the cost of the steamer.

George Wiley, a prominent manufacturer and an active member of the company, instantly arose and said: "I will give another hundred." Others followed and in a few minutes over fourteen hundred dollars was pledged by those present, making, with the sum offered by the company, $2,400. Everything seemed to indicate the purchase of the "Mary Ann" or a similar machine, but the rebellion broke out soon afterwards, and in the earnest efforts made by the Paterson firemen in common with their fellow-workers all over the North to advance the cause of the Union, the plans for purchasing a steam engine were lost sight of and the matter was allowed to drop, as in a short time No. 3's ranks were so depleted by the members enlisting that the company was compelled to appeal to the citizens, asking them to join the company and in that way make up their numbers to an effective force.

Paterson had at that time several crack militia companies, but they did not volunteer with greater alacrity than the firemen. Engine Co. No. 1 had forty-two members. Underneath the names of twenty-eight in the due book are written these words: "Absent in defense of his country." That company's runners (the Passaic Association) enlisted almost to a man. Engine companies 2 and 3 furnished two full companies for the 25th Regt. New Jersey Volunteers; Co. A, Captain John McKiernan, and Co. C, Captain Archibald Graham, the former mainly composed of engine 3's men and the latter made up from members of No. 2. Andrew Derrom, colonel of the 25th, was an old fireman, having served nine years in No. 2, and nearly every line officer in the regiment had seen service as a fireman. Every company recruited in Paterson had in its ranks many firemen, while Co. K, 13th Regt. Volunteers, had for its captain Hugh C. Irish, for many years one of No. 1's most active members. The part taken by Paterson firemen in suppressing the rebellion is a grand one. It has never been written, but when it is made the subject of the historian's pen it will be found an interesting theme. As the war progressed and promotion followed bravery, the fire companies whose members were thus advanced were in the habit of presenting them with the paraphernalia pertaining to the rank conferred. The files of the daily papers frequently contained accounts of presentations to fortunate officers.

James McKiernan, of No. 4, was elected Chief Engineer in April, 1861, enlisted in the following September, and came home major of the 7th New Jersey infantry, his duties as chief being performed for the balance of his term, while he was absent at the front, by his assistants.

With the exception of a few weeks in winter when the snow lay deep, and for two or three days about the Fourth of July, the apparatus was drawn by hand. The question of the use of horses was an ever fresh topic of discussion amongst the firemen, as it was generally supposed that a paid force would follow close upon the heels of the horses. There is little doubt that this feeling had much to do with the delay, although all admit now that it was a mistake to suppose that the volunteer department would go to pieces with rapidity.

The introduction of horses into the department permanently dates back to May, 1884, at which time Passaic Engine Co., No. 1, purchased at its own expense a team of bay horses for its steamer. In August of the same year another horse was bought by the company for the hose cart.

William H. Whittaker was appointed driver of the engine, and for the first six months after the hose cart horse was bought a detail of six members acted as call drivers. In the spring of 1885 Cornelius F. O'Neil was appointed to drive the hose cart. In August, 1885, the city authorities purchased teams for engines 3, 4, and 5, and truck 2. Christopher Cubby, Patrick Sweeny, William Cook and Martin Brandt were appointed drivers, and John Weber was given the position of tillerman. In the summer of 1886 horses were furnished for the hose wagons of engines 4 and 5, the hose cart of engine 3, and truck 1. Peter Riley, William Stannard, Daniel W. Leonard and David McAllister were appointed drivers, and Thomas Elvin tillerman. The following year engines 2, 6, 7, 8, and 9, were given teams, and John Breen, Allison Roswell, Alfred Rogers, John Ellis and Michael Condon were appointed to the position of drivers. In October, 1888, Michael Farrell, of engine 9, was appointed permanent substitute driver and placed in charge of the chief's gig. The pay of the permanent men was $720.00 per annum until 1887, when it was made $850.00 per year.

At the fire which destroyed Allen, Reynolds & Co.'s tobacco factory in Van Houten street, in November, 1865, Patrick Brophy, of engine company No. 3, was buried in the ruins and killed, and James Johnson, engine No. 5, was overcome with the heat at the fire at the Danforth Locomotive Works, July 8th, 1866, and died in a few hours.

Previous to 1868 the leather hose was slushed at each engine house. In 1868 the present city hose house in Bridge street was erected and the firemen were relieved from the disagreeable task of slushing. In 1871 the first rubber hose was purchased, and in 1881 the first lot of cotton hose went into service. The Gamewell fire alarm telegraph was introduced in 1872-73, going into service March 1st, 1873, with twenty-three street boxes, three tower bell strikers, six gongs, one three-circuit repeater and seventeen miles of wire. Edward Gore was the first superintendent of fire alarm. His successors have been Edward Swift, William Hobson and James F. Zeluff. From 1821 to 1838 the wardens appointed the chief and assistant engineers. In 1838 and 1839 the wardens appointed upon nominations made by the firemen, and from 1840 down to the present time they have elected their officers with the exception of James Radcliffe, who was appointed assistant engineer by the board of aldermen in the spring of 1869. The first salary paid was to Chief Lane in 1839, and was $50 per annum. The assistants were not paid until 1851, when they were given $25 yearly salary. The companies are now paid as follows: Engine Co. No. 1 (independent, owning their apparatus and horses), $2,175.00; eight other engine companies, $675 each; two truck companies, $340.00 each; three hose companies, $300.00 each; engine companies are allowed fifty men each, truck companies forty men each, and hose companies thirty men each. Horses were introduced in the department in May, 1884, and sliding poles in 1885.

CHAPTER III.

CHIEFS AND ASSISTANT ENGINEERS.

Past and Present Department Commanders—A Roster of Well-known Names—Date of Appointment and Term of Service.

THE following is an almost complete list of the chief and assistant engineers of the Paterson fire department, with date of appointment: 1821, February 7th, Timothy B. Crane, chief; 1821, December 28th, Samuel Colt, chief. At the same meeting Mr. Colt's election was reconsidered. 1822, January 4th, the wardens voted to serve as chief monthly in alphabetical order. 1823, March 22d, Timothy B. Crane, chief; 1824, January 5th, Timothy B. Crane, chief; 1825, December 9th, Timothy B. Crane, chief; John Rutan and Andrew Parsons, assistant engineers. 1826, December 6th, Timothy B. Crane, chief; 1827, December 10th, Andrew Parsons, chief; John Rutan, assistant engineer. 1828, November 14th, Andrew Parsons, chief; John G. Bates, first assistant; David Reid, second assistant. As Mr. Bates declined to serve, Dec. 1st, Mr. Reid was appointed first assistant and Cornelius S. Post second assistant. 1829, November 2d, John G. Bates, chief; Peter F. Merselis, assistant engineer. Mr. Merselis declining, November 9th, John Garrison was appointed first assistant and

Charles D. Clinton second assistant. 1830, no record of appointments. 1831, November 7th. Josiah M. Crismond, chief; Horatio Moses, first assistant; John H. Ryerson, second assistant. 1832, November 23d, John G. Bates, chief; Alexander Paul, first assistant; Albert Hopper, second assistant. 1833, November 5th, John Sloat, chief; Cornelius H. Post, first assistant; Nathaniel Lane, second assistant. 1834, November 4th, Nathaniel Lane, chief (Lane resigned March 9th, 1835); Cornelius H. Post, first assistant; Henry Van Houten, second assistant. 1835, November 18th, Cornelius Speer, chief; Giles Van Ness, first assistant; Henry Van Houten, second assistant. 1836, December 30th, Horatio Moses, chief. 1837, January 9th, John G. Bates, chief; Nathaniel Lane, first assistant; Albert I. Hopper, second assistant. 1837, November 8th, John G. Bates, chief; Nathaniel Lane, first assistant; Cornelius V. W. Post, second assistant. 1838, November 14th, Nathaniel Lane, chief; Edward McKeon, first assistant; Robert Fields, second assistant. 1839, November 15th, Nathaniel Lane, chief; John Bentley, first assistant; Giles Van Ness, second assistant. On March 27th, 1840, Messrs. Bentley and Van Ness resigned and the wardens appointed William Masters first assistant and Jacob Van Houten second assistant. 1840, November 11th, William Cundell, chief; Titus Ward, first assistant; Cornelius H. Post, second assistant. 1841, William Cundell, chief, no date of election. 1842, Nathaniel Lane, chief; John Benson, first assistant; Cornelius Westervelt, second assistant. 1843, Nathaniel Lane, chief; Alfred Westervelt, first assistant; Peter B. Westervelt, second assistant. 1844, Nathaniel Lane, chief; Austin McCloud, first assistant; Robert Smith, second assistant. 1845, John W. Ackerson, chief, no date of election. 1846, Nathaniel Lane, chief, no date of election. 1847, Nathaniel Lane, chief, no date of election. 1848, May, Thomas O. Smith, chief; Michael B. Murphy, first assistant; Richard B. Chiswell, second assistant. 1849, ——1850,——1851, May 29th, Thomas O. Smith, chief; Patrick Curran, first assistant. There being a tie vote no election was had for second assistant. 1852, Thomas O. Smith, chief; Patrick Curran, first assistant; Griffith King, second assistant. 1853, Patrick Curran, chief; William Douglass, first assistant; Thomas Farnon, second assistant. 1854, Thompson Titus, chief; Thomas Farnon, first assistant. 1855, William Sykes, chief; John Bowering, James A. King, assistants. 1856, William Sykes, chief; John Bowering, James A. King, assistants. 1857, John Bowering, chief; James A. King and Thomas Farnon, assistants. 1858, John Bowering, chief; William Killen and Thomas Farnon, assistants. 1859, James A. King, chief; Jonathan W. Hockett and William Killen, assistants. 1860, James A. King, chief; John Gillespie and James McClory, assistants. 1861, James McKiernan, chief; George J. Bunce and Peter Fields, assistants. 1862, Peter Fields, chief; John McKiernan and John Hinchliffe, assistants. 1863, William Killen, chief; John Schoonmaker and Jacob Pfitzmeir, assistants. 1864, William Killen, chief; Edward Swift and Jacob Pfitzmeir, assistants. 1865, Edward

Swift, chief; George W. Steed and Lawrence Ryan, assistants. 1866, Daniel McClory, chief; Andrew Moser and Charles Reed, assistants. 1867, Andrew Moser, chief; Joseph Bousseleth and Dewitt C. Simonton, assistants. 1868, John McKiernan, chief; Patrick Sweeney and George Young, assistants. 1869, Patrick Sweeney, chief; Edward Gore, William E. Helmrich and Jas. Radcliffe, assistants. 1870, Edward Gore, chief; James Doherty, George Burton and James Atchison, assistants. 1871, James Atchison, chief; Patrick Chapman, William Martin and Thomas Mullen, assistants. 1872, William Martin, chief; Edward Fanning, George M. Case and Thomas Mullen, assistants. 1873, James I. King, chief for two years; assistants, William Bailey, two years; Joseph Buckley, one year. James I. King was the first chief elected for a term of two years. Bailey and Buckley, assistant engineers elect, drew lots to see who would have the two-year term. Bailey was the fortunate man. Thereafter the chiefs and assistants were elected for two years. 1874, Bartholomew Reilly, assistant. 1875, John E. Regner, chief; Fredrick Wieler, assistant. 1876, Lambert Romaine, assistant. 1877, David I. Turnbull, chief; William Bland, assistant. 1878, Patrick Morrison, assistant. 1879, Bartholomew Reilly, chief; Gustave Specht, assistant. 1880, James Kearney, assistant. 1881, Leonard Garrison, chief; Daniel W. Leonard, assistant. 1882, Louis Brandt, assistant. 1883, John MacDonald, chief; Peter Zeluff, assistant. 1884, Samuel S. Pounds, assistant. 1885, James Kearney, chief; Charles Carroll, assistant. 1886, Frank W. King, assistant. 1887, John Stagg, chief; John Struck, assistant. 1888, John Crotty, assistant.

CHAPTER IV.

ENGINE AND HOSE COMPANY SKETCHES.

When Organized and Where Located—The Goose-neck and Piano-box Engines—The Amoskeag—The Silsby—Modern Apparatus—Hose and Hook and Ladder Companies.

PASSAIC Engine Co., No. 1, was organized July 4th, 1815. The first location of which we have any knowledge was in a small, one-story frame building on the north side of Van Houten street, east of Prospect street, which was occupied until January, 1843, when the house was burned down. They then were housed in the old house of Engine Co. No. 2 on Market street, opposite Prospect street, until the latter part of February of the same year, when they removed to a two-story frame building on the corner of Broadway and Mulberry street. This house sheltered them until the spring of 1853, at which time they took possession of a two-story brick building adjoining their old quarters. Here they were stationed until 1871. In May of that year they removed to their present commodious quarters, No. 112 Van Houten street. The first engine used by the company was a cumbersome affair operated by hand brakes and a roller, underneath the box, upon which the rope was wound. In May, 1822, an engine was purchased from Sayre & Force, of New York. This was a side brake engine. In June, 1835, the famous Black Hawk, a goose-neck machine built by James Smith, of New York, was received by the company. In March, 1853, they procured a Van Ness engine, piano-box style. This machine was so heavy that in 1855 a Smith piano-box engine was purchased and was used until May, 1866. In December, 1865, the company purchased an unfinished single pump Banks steamer in New York. It was completed in the engine house and went in service the following May. This machine did duty until September, 1874, at which time Harrell & Hayes, of Paterson, N. J., built a double pump engine for them at a cost of $5,000. This did good service until January, 1886, when they bought their present apparatus (a Button steamer). This company was the first to introduce horses in the department, in 1884; the sliding pole, in 1885, and the steam heater in 1886.

NEPTUNE ENGINE CO. NO. 2.

This company was organized in December, 1820. Their first engine was a goose-neck built by Smith, of New York. In 1840 they received a new goose-neck engine built by James Smith. Their next engine was a piano-box machine built by William Jeffers, of Pawtucket, R. I., and delivered February 22d, 1864. In February, 1872, the company purchased at their own expense a double pump steam fire engine. The company was out of service for several months during 1875. In July, 1876, they were given a double pump steamer built by Joseph Nussey, of Paterson, They used this engine until the spring of 1883, when the city authorities bought and put in their charge the Jeffers steamer formerly run by them. The company were first housed in a shed on the south side of Market street, east of Main. Later they occupied a one-story frame house lower down the street, opposite Prospect street. Here they remained until 1842, when they removed to their present location on Hotel street. Five years later they were burned out, but the house was immediately rebuilt.

Washington Engine Co. No. 3.

This company was organized and placed in service April 20th, 1828, in a two-story brick and stone building on the west side of Washington street, below Fair street. Their first engine was a goose-neck engine built by Ephraim Force, of New York. In 1836 the engine was removed to a frame building on Ellison street, south side, near Prospect street. In July, 1848, the house burned down and a two-story brick building was built for them. They remained at this spot until 1856, when they removed to their present quarters on Prospect street. They ran their goose-neck until 1856, when they received a piano-box engine built by James Smith, of New York. In July, 1864, a single pump Jeffers steam engine was placed in their charge. This was the first steamer used in Paterson. In September, 1881, a second-class double pump Amoskeag engine was purchased for the company and is now being used by them.

Phœnix Engine Co. No. 4.

This company was organized September 12th, 1828. Their apparatus was the double decker owned by the Phœnix Manufacturing Co., and during the brief existence of the company they were quartered in a two-story frame building on the south side of Bondinot (now Van Houten) street. Their machine was the only double decker ever in service in this city, and the membership, as a rule, was composed of persons in the employ of the Phœnix corporation. Each member was provided with a white duck coat, which hung on a peg in the engine house. The question of who was to pay sundry bills incurred by the company was the cause of frequent debates at meetings of the fire wardens, and finally, on August 11th, 1842, the wardens notified the company that their services were no longer needed, and their connection with the fire department of the Town of Paterson was severed.

JACKSON ENGINE CO. No. 4.

This company was organized and placed in service in the fall of 1855. Their first engine was a piano-box engine built by James Smith, of New York. A two-story brick house was built for them on Slater street, near Jersey, where they are still located. They ran the Smith engine until Thanksgiving Day, 1868, when they received a new steamer from the Paterson Steam Fire Engine Works, which was the first fire engine built in Paterson. Their present steamer (a Clapp & Jones) was delivered to them in 1882.

PROTECTION ENGINE CO. No. 5.

This company was organized in the spring of 1832 and went into service with a Smith goose-neck engine. They lay at the southwest corner of High and Temple streets.

They were burned out in 1856 and 1860. In 1861 their present quarters were erected for them. In 1865 the company received, in place of their first and only goose-neck engine, a piano-box machine built by John N. Dennison, of Newark, N. J. This was run by them until November, 1870, when they were given a third-class double pump engine built by the Paterson Steam Fire Engine Works. In 1884 they received their present Silsby engine.

Engine Co. No. 6.

When a new goose-neck engine was purchased for Neptune No. 2, in the spring of 1840, their old engine was placed in charge of a new company which was stationed at the corner of Broadway and Mulberry streets. The company was short-lived, never having over thirteen members, and they were disbanded December 6, 1842.

Vigilant Engine Co. No. 6.

This company was organized January 1st, 1867. They were given the hand engine last used by Engine Co. No. 1, and were housed in a one-story frame building which stood on a lot adjoining their present quarters, where they lay until the brick house was quilt for them. In the fall of 1871 they were furnished with a third-class double pump steamer, built by the Paterson works. In the winter of 1887 their present Clapp & Jones engine came.

Lexington Engine Co. No. 7.

This company was instituted in 1868. The company was composed of residents of Totowa, and their engine was the Smith machine used by Engine No. 3 at the time the latter company's Jeffers steamer came. They were quar-

JAMES C. MILLS,
ASSISTANT CHIEF.

tered in a one-story frame building at the corner of Sheridan avenue and Henry street. The company was soon disbanded. Their last appearance in public was on a Saturday afternoon, when they took their engine to "Molly Ann's" brook for a "wash" and left her there.

LIBERTY ENGINE CO. NO. 7.

This company was organized August 9th, 1871, and went into service in April, 1872. Their first engine was a piano-box engine, formerly used by Engine No. 6. They were first located in a one-story frame building on the lot where their present quarters are situated. In September, 1879, their present engine, a single pump Clapp & Jones, was put in service.

LAFAYETTE ENGINE CO. NO. 8.

This company was instituted in 1872, going into service in August of that year. They first ran from a one-story frame building located on Sherman avenue, near Totowa avenue. They were given the engine which Lexington No. 7 had used. Their next location was at the corner of Wayne avenue and Liberty street, where they are now located. The city fathers placed in their charge in September, 1874, a double pump engine built by the Paterson works. Their present house, a two-story brick one, was built in 1876.

PATERSON ENGINE CO. NO. 9.

This company was organized in 1882 and went on duty March 3d, 1883, with No. 2's old Nussey engine, which they still run. They were first housed in a brick building at the corner of Jackson street and Washington avenue.

They took possession of their present quarters in February, 1884.

Columbia Hose Co. No. 1.

This company was organized in April, 1855. Their first apparatus was a four-spring carriage with three bells. The company were first quartered in John (now Ellison) street, between Engine No. 3 and Truck No. 1, for a few months, until their present home in Broadway was built. Their house was furnished in a handsome and costly manner. At a fight which occurred in the fall of 1856 two members of Hose No. 1 joined Engine No. 5's men in resisting an attack from Engine No. 4's men, and as a result they were expelled from the department and Engine Co. No. 5 disbanded. Hose No. 1 demanded a fair trial for their expelled brothers. This being refused they voluntarily disbanded and ended their career by a supper at John Walden's Washington Hotel. A new company went into service January 16th, 1857. On July 4th, 1864, the company received their present carriage from William Jeffers, of Pawtucket, R. I.

Cataract Hose Co. No. 2.

This company was organized June 10th, 1869, and went into service December 1st of that year. The city purchased of Thomas Peto, of Philadelphia, the carriage now run by them. The company was quartered in Engine No. 1's house until July 10th, 1870, when they took possession of their new house at the corner of Auburn and Goodwin streets.

Hibernia Hose Co. No. 3.

This company was organized in 1869, and went into service February 1st, 1870. Their carriage was built by Nichols & Co., at the Paterson Steam Fire Engine Works. It is the same style of carriage as Hose No. 2. The city erected a house for them upon the lot adjoining Engine No. 4's house, where they are still quartered.

Eagle Hook and Ladder Co. No. 1.

This company was organized and placed in service March 22d, 1839. July 23d, 1848, their house on Ellison street, next to No. 3's house, was burned down, and a small two-story brick house was built for them upon the same site. In 1856 they went into new quarters on Prospect street. August 4th, 1858, they received a new goose-neck reach truck from Pine & Partshorn, of New York, which they ran until February 22d, 1872, when they were given a light truck built in Brooklyn, N. Y., and the year following they went to their present house on Jackson street. In July, 1880, their house, apparatus and furniture were burned up. Their house was immediately re-built, but they did not receive their present apparatus until September, 1881.

Germania Hook and Ladder Co. No. 2.

This company was instituted in the fall of 1871. They went into service April 1st, 1872, using the old Eagle truck and running from a shed in the rear of old Military Hall, corner of Cross and Ellison streets, until they occupied the old Eagle truck house in Prospect street in 1873. Their present truck was placed in service in December, 1882-

CHAPTER V.

A CITY ORDINANCE, 1875.

Providing for the Regulation, Management and Government of the Department—Elections, How Conducted—Officers and Elections—Duties and Responsibilities.

WE now approach a period when the history of the fire department rests upon recorded and authenticated facts, as revealed in the successive annual reports of the Chief Engineer, and in the laws and ordinances. So far the story has been followed as recorded in the published sketch mentioned in the preface. The present writer takes up the history where it has been dropped, and continues it to the present in consecutive form.

An ordinance for the general regulation, management and government of the fire department of the city of Paterson, passed April 9th, 1875, provided that each fire engine company might have, but should not exceed, seventy-five members; that each hook and ladder company might have, but should not exceed, sixty members; that each hose company might have, but should not exceed, sixty members.

That the election for Chief Engineer and two Assistant Engineers of the fire department should be held on the first Tuesday after the first Monday in May, 1875, between the hours of 7 and 9 o'clock in the afternoon, at the house of each company, and the person so elected Chief Engineer should hold office for the term of two years from the 20th day of May, 1875, and his successor should be elected, in the manner above provided, on the first Tuesday after the first Monday in May, every two years thereafter. And the two Assistant Engineers so elected should one of them hold his office for the term of two years; and there should be elected one Assistant Engineer on the first Tuesday after the first Monday in May every year thereafter; and the two Assistant Engineers so to be elected should determine by lot which should hold the office for the term of two years.

There should be elected by each company at such election one Judge of Election and one Clerk, who should possess the same qualifications and perform the same duties at the said elections as near as might be for city officers, Judges of Election and Ward Clerks, who should before entering upon the duties of their respective offices take an oath or affirmation faithfully and impartially to perform all the duties of their offices according to law.

Every duly qualified member of the department should be entitled to vote in person at any such election, at the engine house of the company of which he was at that time an active member.

That it should be the duty of the Chief Engineer, together with the Assistant Engineers, in case of fire. to see that the several fire engines, and the apparatus thereto belonging, were worked and used in the most effectual manner for the extinguishment of the same; and to enforce the observance of good order among the members of the several fire companies while on duty.

It was their duty also to examine the several fire engines, and the hose and apparatus thereto belonging, at least once in every two weeks, and to examine into the condition of all hydrants, and if any of the same were deficient, to designate the same particularly, and to report thereon once in each month.

To each company organized and enrolled according to law, there should be one Foreman, one Assistant Foreman and Secretary; to be elected annually by the foremen of the company, and each to hold his office for one year, and until his successor was elected.

All members of the Paterson Fire Department should, when on duty as firemen, wear the leather cap as hitherto used, or a badge as provided.

That each enrolled company shall, as compensation therefor, in quarter-yearly payments, in lieu of all and every other charge or demand of any kind whatever, receive the following named sums per year, to wit: To Engine Companies Nos. 1 and 2, each, $1,000; to Engine Companies Nos. 3, 4, 5, 6 and 8, each $500; Engine Company No. 7, $400; each Hook and Ladder Company, $340; each Hose Company, $300.

The foregoing are the leading features of the ordinance.

CHAPTER VI.

DIGEST OF SOME ANNUAL REPORTS.

Views of the Mayor and Chief Engineer—Looking toward a Paid Fire Department—Recommending the purchase of a Steam Fire Engine—The last Hand Engine.

THERE is, as has been said, solid and sufficient historical material of the fire and police departments from 1875 to date, thanks to the printed annual reports of the city officers. From these reports the following chapters have been compiled.

1876.—Mayor Benjamin Buckley, in his annual report, said that no city could be considered safe without a properly organized and well-disciplined fire department. There was a great difference of opinion among the people, whether under the volunteer system, as then organized, an effective fire department could be obtained. There were many citizens, whose opinions were entitled to great weight, who contended strongly for a paid fire department. He did not think that the time had come when tax-payers were ready to approve of increasing the current expenses of the city to that extent which would be necessary to maintain a paid fire department. Assuming such to be the fact, efforts should be directed towards making the existing department as effective as possible. He had recently visited, with the

Chief Engineer, all the engine houses in the city, and examined carefully the different steamers, trucks, and hose carriages, together with the hose, and was glad to say that he found them, as a rule, in good condition.

Chief Engineer John E. Regner's report showed that during the year ending May 1st, 1876, there had been forty-six fires, five still alarms and two false alarms. The losses by fire and water amounted to $312,130.00, insurance, $273,430.00.

The Department consisted of the following companies and apparatus:

Passaic Steamer, No. 1; Washington Steamer, No. 3; Jackson Steamer, No. 4; Protection Steamer, No. 5; Vigilant Steamer, No. 6; Lafayette Steamer, No. 8; Liberty Hand Engine, No. 7; Eagle Hook & Ladder, No. 1; Germania Hook & Ladder, No. 2; Columbia Hose Carriage, No. 1; Cataract Hose Carriage, No. 2; Hibernia Hose Carriage, No. 3; Neptune Hose Carriage, No. 2.

In service, 4,000 feet of good rubber hose, 4,500 feet of leather hose, in poor condition. The apparatus in charge of the department was in good order with the exception of Steamer No. 4 and Steamer No. 5. He recommended the purchase of another steamer. An additional steamer would enable them to have at all times a sufficient force for any emergency.

1877.—The recommendation of the Mayor in the previous message for the building of a new house for Company No. 8; also the purchase of a new steamer for Company No. 2, and the repairing of the house in Jackson street, had been adopted during the past year. Application had been been made for a new house for Engine Company, No. 7.

The manual force of the department consisted of 1 Chief Engineer, 2 Assistant Engineers, 508 members of engine companies, 137 members of hose companies, and 92 members of hook and ladder companies. Total, 737.

The Chief reported the department in a good working condition, and the discipline worthy of all praise.

The Mayor said he believed that the department was not excelled by any volunteer deparment in the country.

1878.—During the year there were 46 fires and 35 alarms by telegraph, entailing a loss of $39,512 of property.

The manual force of the department consisted of 1 Chief Engineer, 2 Assistant Engineers, 525 members of engine companies, 102 members of truck companies, 120 members of hose companies. Total, 750.

The apparatus consisted of seven steam fire engines and tenders, one hand engine and hose cart, two hook and ladder trucks, three hose carriages and one supply wagon; all in fair working condition.

The department had experienced a great deal of trouble with defective hose, which had all been tested and repaired, with indifferent success.

1879.—Mayor Graham, in his annual report, recommended that a new steam fire engine be purchased for the use of Engine Company, No. 7, Tyler street, as the hand engine was useless.

The totals are as follows: number of fires, 44; loss, $258,487; insurance on loss, $124,468.

The efficiency of the department, the Mayor said, and the faithfulness of its members, were matters of record.

1880.—The Mayor, as usual, was eulogistic in his report of the workings of the department.

During the past year the department had been increased by the purchase of a new steamer for No. 7 Company. This dispensed with the last hand engine in the department, bringing the number of steamers up to eight.

All the steamers were small and lightly built, and the Mayor recommended that a large, first-class engine be purchased, to be located in the house of one of those companies situated in the center of the city, where it would do the most effectual work; also, that a steamer be placed in the southern part of the city, as, from the construction of the buildings in that section, there was great danger of a large destruction of property should a fire occur.

The whole cost of the department during the year was $31,279.57.

The fire department telegraph, under the management of the present superintendent, was in good condition and had generally done its work satisfactorily. But with the utmost care on the part of the superintendent, failures would occur, which might be attributed to the wires of the department being in collision with other boxes.

New signal boxes were from time to time added in localities needing them, as frequency of alarm stations enhanced the chances for early alarms.

1882.—The special committee appointed to perfect a fire escape ordinance had never been able to make a report. It was deemed important that such a limit should be established; also, a Bureau of Permits, where all plans for new buildings should be submitted for approval before they could be erected. Fire escapes had been placed on most of the large factories, and steps taken to perfect the ordinance bearing on this subject.

The manual force of the department consisted of 1 Chief Engineer, 2 Assistant Engineers, 572 members of engine companies, 148 members of hose companies, and 109 members of truck companies; making a total membership of 832.

1883.—The Mayor recommended that the ordinances of the city in regard to fire limits should be so made that they would operate uniformly. Unless a uniform rule was enforced there would never have been buildings of brick or stone in the thickly settled part of the city. Horses should also be purchased for a portion of the fire engines, so that in case of emergency the engines might be rapidly taken to fires.

CHAPTER VII.

DISAPPEARANCE OF THE HAND ENGINE.

Employment of Horses for Moving of Engines—Improved Steam Apparatus—Membership of the Department—Fires and Alarms—Chief Stagg Complimented.

IN 1884 the Mayor complained in his message that a class of buildings was being thrust upon the city in violation of the ordinance concerning fire limits. Permits had been granted continually for altering and enlarging the tinder-boxes within these limits. The schools, churches and halls should be provided with fire escapes, and the strength of the walls ascertained.

During the year there had been 37 bell alarms, and 8 still alarms.

Chief MacDonald recommended the purchase of a new steam fire engine for Protection Steam Fire Engine Company, No. 5; also, a new tender for Paterson Steam Fire Engine Company, No. 9.

During the year a new engine house had been built at South Paterson, for Engine Company, No. 9, and a new steam fire engine bought for Engine Company, No. 4.

The force of the department consisted of 1 Chief Engineer, 2 Assistant Engineers, 613 members of engine companies, 137 members of hose companies, and 102 members of truck companies. Total, 852.

The apparatus consisted of nine steam engines, nine four-wheel tenders, three hose carriages, and two hook and ladder trucks; one steam engine, old No. 4, held in reserve at the hose house, and one supply wagon.

Totals: fires, 45; damage, $80,223.38; insurance, $305,-092.00.

1885.—The Mayor expressed himself as of the opinion that the fire department should have, wherever practicable, horses for the moving of the engines. The delay of a few minutes in dragging an engine to a fire that might break out in the mills of the city where light fabrics were made or kept, might be great enough to cause an amount of loss that would justify the city in a moderate expenditure for horses to facilitate the movement of some of the steamers.

It would not be necessary, he said, that all engine houses should be thus equipped at once or in the near future. The great efficiency of the volunteer department was universally recognized.

There were located for fire purposes up to and including March 1st, 1885, 591 fire hydrants, an increase of 36 during the year.

The apparatus consisted of nine steam fire engines, nine four-wheel tenders, three hose carriages, and two hook and ladder trucks, and one supply wagon.

During the year there had been 77 fires and alarms, showing an increase over the previous year of 32, of which there were 66 bell alarms, an increase of 29. There were 11 still, an increase of 3.

The city has grown so rapidly of late years, there was an actual necessity for the speedy conveyance of the fire apparatus to the scene of action; and this required the equipment of horses for some of the fire companies; a state of affairs brought to the attention of the Mayor and Board of Aldermen by Chief John MacDonald.

1886.—The foregoing recommendations of the Chief were endorsed by Mayor Beckwith in his annual message. He, also, favored the purchase of horses, and whenever steamers were to be bought to replace old ones, or as an increase in the established number, they should, he said, be of the most ample power and of the first quality.

The force of the department consisted of 1 Chief Engineer, 2 Assistant Chief Engineers, 571 members of engine companies, 121 members of hose companies, 100 members of hook and ladder companies, making a total membership of 792 men.

The apparatus consisted of nine steam fire engines, nine four-wheel tenders, three hose carriages and two hook and ladder trucks, and one supply wagon.

There were, besides, of old apparatus, two steam fire engines, one old No. 4, stored in Eagle Truck House, Jackson street, and one old No. 5, stored in the Hose House shed, Bridge street. Also, one old four-wheel tender in the same shed.

The various engine, hose, and hook and ladder houses were in very good condition, with the exception of Engine

Companies Nos. 4, 7 and 8, which were greatly troubled with the water in their cellars most of the year round. The horses were all doing well, and improving in their work, and the Chief recommended to have two sets of shoes and have a man to come and put them on in their several houses whenever required.

1887.—The Mayor again adverted to the necessity of purchasing more horses. Nos. 2, 6, 7, 8 and 9 should, he said, have horses, if possible.

The various engine, truck and hose houses were in pretty fair condition. A slight alteration to the house of Truck No. 1 was needed, the raising of the door one foot higher; the water closets in the houses of Hose No. 3 and Engine No. 9 needed to be altered, and new ones put in and properly ventilated; the back wall of the house of Engine No. 5 had settled; the cellar of Engine No. 7's house contained water all the year round, but was in a good condition every other way.

During the year there had been 84 fires and alarms, an increase of 3 over previous year. There were 77 bell alarms and 7 still alarms.

The Chief recommended the purchase of a new hose wagon for Engine Company No. 6, as the one they had was past its day of usefulness. He also said that the drivers and tillermen were not paid in proportion to the time; they had long hours, and he would be pleased to see their pay increased. He advocated the placing of heaters in the houses of Engine Companies Nos. 3 and 4, and in all houses where it was intended to put horses; also, the appointment of a permanent engineer in the same. He also recommended the purchase of three thousand feet of first-class Fabric hose, which, with proper care, would outlast the rubber hose; and tenders could carry more of Fabric than of rubber hose. There was not a full quantity of good hose to give two changes, which every first-class city had.

1888.—The Mayor paid a tribute to the efficiency of the department, as evidenced by the report of the Chief Engineer, John Stagg. He was rejoiced that his recommendations had been carried out, resulting in giving all the steamers horses.

The members of the Fire Department could be divided into four classes, viz: Permanent men, 18; partly paid or call men, 21; officers of companies, 40; members of companies, 596—making a total of 675. Of these 511 were attached to engines; 74 to trucks; and 90 to hose companies. The permanent men consisted of Superintendent of Fire Alarm, 9 drivers of engines; 2 drivers of trucks; 4 drivers of hose wagons or hose carriages, and 2 tillermen. The call men consisted of Chief Engineer and 2 Assistants, and 18 engineers for steamers.

The annual salary of the above and of the respective companies is as follows: Chief Engineer, $600; Assistant Engineers, $300; Fire Alarm Superintendent, $600; Drivers of engines, wagons and trucks, $750; Tillermen, $750; Steamer Engineers, $887.50; Engine Companies—No. 1,* $2,000; No. 2, $500; No. 3, $500; No. 4, $500; No. 5,

---

* This company owns its apparatus and horses and pays its own drivers out of the allowance named.

W. Cook, Captain.
W. Allen, Captain.

E. J. Coleman, Captain.
W. Boyle, Captain.

$500; No. 6, $500; No. 7, $500; No. 8, $500; No. 9, $500; Truck Companies—No. 1, $340; No. 2, $340; Hose Companies—No. 1, $300; No. 2, $300; No. 3, $300.

CHAPTER VIII.

A PAID FIRE DEPARTMENT.

The Volunteers Are Succeeded by the Present System — Radical Changes — Increased Expenditures — Efficiency of the Service Increased — Modern Methods and Scientific Appliances.

IN the year 1888 the board of aldermen took away from the companies the election of chief and assistant engineers, and in May, 1889, appointed David I. Turnbull chief and John F. Murphy assistant engineer. During that year the department was reorganized by a special committee consisting of Aldermen Macdonald, Miller and Kearney, and a paid department succeeded the volunteer system on March 20th, 1890, with four permanent men in nine engine and three hook and ladder companies, and eight call men to each. John Gillmer succeeded John Crotty as assistant engineer in May, 1890. Chief Turnbull resigned May 5th, 1890, and Assistant John Murphy was appointed to fill vacancy of term. John Struck succeeding Assistant Murphy. The Legislature, in the spring of 1891, passed a law making the office of chief and assistant engineers during good behavior, and in May, 1891, John Stagg was elected chief and James Mills assistant engineer. In June, 1891, Assistant John Gillmer resigned and was reappointed under the law of 1891.

The first break into the volunteer system was the disbanding of the three hose companies in the spring of 1890, and the formation of a new truck company known as Rapid H. & L. No. 3, which was located in quarters of Cataract Hose No. 3.

Paterson was well pleased with the old volunteers, as no other band of men in any section of the country did their duty more faithfully, but the reorganization on a paid system was brought about by the increased duty of the men and the necessary taking, at the time of fires, of so many from the shops and factories.

1889.—There were in the department 9 steam fire engines. A partially paid fire department and the organization of "call" men was earnestly recommended; also the purchase of a chemical engine and that three steam engines be dispensed with; it being conceded by fire authorities that six steamers and one chemical engine would be more practical as well as economical, if the department be organized with call men, similar to the Newark system.

During the year the department had answered 141 alarms of fire. The loss on buildings, $43,875.50; insurance, $278,500.00. Loss on stock, etc., $65,217.90; insurance, $128,320.00. Total loss, $109,093.40; insurance, $406,520.00.

The members of the department, divided into four classes, were as follows, viz: Permanent men, 19; partly paid, 21; officers of companies, 41; members of companies. 555. Permanent men consisted of superintendent of fire alarm, nine drivers of engines, two drivers of trucks, four drivers of hose wagons or carriages, two tillermen and one extra driver. The call men consisted of the chief, two assistants, and eighteen engineers for engines. The salaries of the above and the companies per annum were as follows:

Chief engineer, $600; assistant engineers, $300; fire alarm superintendent, $600; drivers of engines, wagons and trucks, $750; tillermen, $750; steam engineers, $85; engine companies—No. 1, $500; No. 2, $500; No. 3, $500; No. 4, $500; No. 5, $500; No. 6, $500; No. 7, $500; No. 8, $500; No. 9, $500; truck companies—No. 1, $340; No. 2, $340; hose companies—No. 1, $300; No. 2, $300; No. 3, $300.

1890.—The radical change made from a volunteer to a paid system would, Mayor Burnett thought, eventually bring about the dispensing with some of the engines. He suggested that one chemical engine, with five or six steamers, would suffice.

On March 20th the department was reorganized by appointing four permanent and eight call men to each company. To the department, with the knowledge of their disbandment, the chief engineer said he appreciated the earnestness and zeal which the department evinced in their services to the public during the past year under the contumely which always seems part of the reward of a volunteer.

A review of this department for the past year would be partly as follows:

Horses, hose wagons, etc., bought; drivers appointed in engine companies Nos. 2, 6 and 7; horses bought for hose carriages in engine companies Nos. 8 and 9; heaters bought for engines Nos. 3, 4 and 6; Babcock ærial truck bought for truck company No. 1; organization of truck company No. 3, with apparatus from truck company No. 1, driver and tillerman appointed, horse and wagon furnished chief; 1,500 feet cotton hose placed in service; 69 hydrants were set during the year, making a total of 784.

1891.—The mayor said in his message that the transition from a volunteer to a paid fire department had necessarily and materially increased the expenditures on this account, so that the money to be raised to avert the dangers of fire formed one of the most important items of the annual tax levy. Although the expense of maintaining the fire department had increased more in proportion than the expenses of other departments of the city government there were still sections of the city inadequately protected. West Paterson, Madison Park, the Eastside and other parts of the city claimed attention; the residents there argued that they were entitled to the same protection accorded to others, just as they paid the same proportion of taxes. Nevertheless, the mayor said, he could not urge the purchase of more apparatus. If the protection afforded by the fire department could be equalized there would be sufficient for the whole territory embraced within the city limits; the difficulty was that in past years engine houses were crowded together in the center of the city and little regard was had for property which was developing in other parts of the city. He would suggest inquiry into the feasibility of removing one or more of the engines from their present location to places where there was greater need of them.

This, in his estimation, could be accomplished with comparatively little expense and the efficiency of the service might be thereby increased.

The total manual force of the department consisted of one chief engineer; two assistant engineers; thirteen captains of companies: ten engineers of steamers; nine drivers of steamers; nine drivers of hose wagons; three drivers of H. & L. trucks; two drivers to chemical engine; one driver to chief engineer; six tillermen of H. & L. trucks; one keeper of hose and coal depot; ninety-six call men, making a total of 153 men.

The apparatus of the department consists of ten steam fire engines and one in reserve, seven hose wagons, two four-wheel hose carts, three hook and ladder trucks, one supply wagon, one chief's wagon.

During the year, one double 60-gallon horizontal Babcock fire extinguisher was purchased and company formed of permanent men formerly connected with engine company No. 2, and went in service September 14, 1890. The chemical engine had been of great service in the extinguishment of fires. Two third size Silsby steamers had been purchased, one for engine company No. 8 and the other for engine company No. 9. One hose wagon had been purchased and placed with engine company No. 8. One three-horse hitch was purchased for No. 1 truck, all of which had been of great service.

Ground was purchased and a new engine house was erected on Highland street. Engine company No. 2 was reorganized and placed on duty there December 1, 1890, with steamer and hose wagon. At that point greater protection from fire had been given to that section of the city known as Riverside.

There were ninety-six bell alarms of fire on the fire alarm telegraph during the year. Of this number four were general and two second alarms.

1892.—The following table shows the manual force of this department, with annual compensation paid:

One chief engineer, $1,500; two assistant engineers, each, $1,000; thirteen captains, each, $900; two engineers of steamers, each, $875; eighteen drivers of steamers and wagons, each, $850; three drivers of trucks, each, $850; two drivers of chemical engine, each, $850; one driver of chief's wagon, $850; six tillermen of H. & L. truck, each, $850; one driver supply wagon, $850; ninety-five hosemen and laddermen at call, $150.

APPOINTMENTS.—1891: John Stagg, chief engineer, May 6; James C. Mills, May 25; John Gillmor, June 1; assistant engineers; Frank Geroe, Feb. 15; Geo. Wassmer, June 15, Geo. V. Brower, Christian Mundrich, Chas. H. McGinnis, July 20; Wm. H. Ward, Sept. 10; Felix McCann, Thomas N. Hallwell, Sept. 21; Archie Irwin, Dec. 7; Wm. Butterworth, Dec. 21. 1892: H. Henry Harding, Feb. 15; John Clark, March 7, callmen.

APPARATUS.—The apparatus consists of nine steam fire engines and one in reserve; eight hose wagons, one four-wheeled hose cart, and one in reserve; three hook and ladder trucks, one of which is an 85-foot Babcock Aerial; one chemical engine, one supply wagon and one chief's wagon.

The truck used by H. & L. Co. No. 3, should, Chief Stagg said in his annual report, be replaced with a new steel frame city truck with all modern appliances, as one now in use is not safe for men to ride on, and ladders are old and rotten, and being constantly repaired.

The value of the Chemical Engine and Extinguishers has been proved to the satisfaction of all, and instead of the purchase of another engine I would recommend that a combination hose and chemical wagon be placed in the houses of Engines Nos. 2 and 9, to be drawn by two horses. This would give the two outlying sections of the city more protection than they now have; also, to place in each of these companies at least two permanent men, and reducing their call force three or four men.

Houses.—All the houses in the department are in good condition except Nos. 6, 9 and Truck No. 3. If the location of Engine No. 6 is not changed, very heavy repairs will be necessary to make it fit for its future use as a fire station. The front of house of Engine No. 9 needs repairing; also, the back and side walls of Truck No. 3. The front doors in house of Truck No. 1 should be made wider, to enable three horses to get out without crowding. Sewer connections should be made at Engine No. 8, if new sewer is laid in Liberty street the coming year.

Horses.—The number of horses in the department at close of year is thirty-nine. Six have been purchased, four condemned and sold, one died of injuries received in pasture field, and one died of disease. At least four new horses should be purchased, and one now at hose house sold, as he is unfit for service in a fire house.

HYDRANTS AND WATER SUPPLY.—Through the kindness of Mr. Wm. Ryle, Superintendent of the Passaic Water Company, says Chief Stagg, I am enabled to present the following: We have now seventy-four miles of pipe laid, consisting of 36, 24, 20, 16, 12, 10, 8, 6 and 4 inch pipe, with 878 fire hydrants. The reservoirs, four in number, have a combined capacity of 47,000,000 gallons, backed by pumping machinery of 24,000,000 gallons daily,

HOSE.—The total amount of hose in the department is 13,800 feet, of the following manufacturers: Fabric Fire Hose Co., Callahan & Co., and Eureka Fire Hose Co.; of which 11,200 feet is in first-class condition, 1,500 feet is in second-class condition, 1,100 feet is in third-class condition; 6,450 feet is laid in wagons on reels, and 7,350 feet in reserve at hose depot; 57,650 feet of hose was used by the department, and afterwards hung up, dried and brushed off. Four hundred feet of hose unfit for service is stored away. At least two thousand feet of new hose should be purchased every year to replace damaged and worn-out stock.

During the year the department had answered to 103 bell alarms and 97 still and telephone alarms, which represents a total loss of $292,278.00, and were insured for $1,162,904.00. Two times alarms were sent out for same fire from different stations. Of 198 calls on department for service at fires, 109 were extinguished by Chemical Engine No. 1, or the small extinguishers carried in hose wagons and trucks; 28 by use of water and chemicals; 15 by water only, and 46 times the department services were not required. The engine companies laid 57,650 feet of hose, through which water was forced by engine. The Chemical Engine used 71 tanks of 60 gallons each, and 195 charges from extinguishers of three and six gallons each were used by other companies.

The department responded to one call outside city lines, by sending an engine, No. 7, to Wortendyke, in charge of Chief Mills.

The fire limit as now established, the Chief maintained, should be enlarged, and the granting of frame buildings inside the limit stopped. Many permits are granted to make repairs which are rebuilding almost entirely of the structures. Many of the cellars, lofts and yards of our largest business houses are nothing but catch-alls for all the inflammable material that can be put away, such as paper, packing cases, barrels, straw, excelsior, etc., and with the large number of lightly built frame structures in the thickly settled portion of our city, it is only a question of time when they will be wiped out by a sweeping conflagration. It is deplorable that some effective effort is not made to have more substantial buildings erected within the boundary lines of a fire limit.

Bell alarms, 303; still alarms, 97; total fires, 200. Insurance, stock and furniture, $517,239; loss, $213,348; insurance, buildings, $645,665; loss, $79,930. Total insurance, $1,162,904; total loss, $292,278.

CHAPTER IX.

PRESENT STATUS OF THE DEPARTMENT.

Officers—Apparatus—Engine, Truck and Hose Companies—The Men and Their Work—How the Companies Are Manned and Officered—Valiant Fire Fighters.

FOR many years, as has been noted, Paterson had one of the best volunteer departments in the country. It is now a paid department, officered as follows: Chief Engineer, John Stagg; First Assistant, James C. Mills; Second Assistant, John Gillmor. Superintendent Fire Alarm Telegraph, James F. Zeluff.

The total manual force of the department consists of one chief engineer, two assistant engineers, thirteen captains of companies, ten engineers of steamers, nine drivers of steamers, nine drivers of hose wagons, three drivers of H. & L. trucks, two drivers of chemical engine, one driver to chief engineer, six tillermen of H. & L. trucks, one keeper of hose and coal depot, ninety-six call men, making a total of 153 men.

APPARATUS.—The apparatus of the department consists of nine steam fire engines and one in reserve, eight hose wagons, one four-wheel hose cart, three hook and ladder trucks, one supply wagon, one chief's wagon.

ENGINE No. 1.—Located on Van Houten street, near

Washington. Engine second size Button, purchased in 1886 and in good condition. Hose wagon built by Gleason & Bailey, carries 800 feet of hose, and in good condition, two 3-gallon extinguishers. Captain, Ernest S. Fields; Engineer, John Knaus; drivers, Arthur Rogers and Samuel Miller; callmen, Wm. J. Post, Wm. H. Brown, Theo. A. Brown, Con. F. O'Neil, Chas. H. McGuinness, Daniel Gregory, Joseph Bachlin, Joseph Hardy.

ENGINE No. 2.—Located on Highland street, near Sassafras. Engine second size Jeffers, purchased in 1871 and in fair condition. Hose wagon, built by John Post, carries 700 feet of hose, and in good condition, two 3-gallon extinguishers. Captain, Floyd King; Engineer, George Dobson; drivers, Henry Nagle and George Sheldrake; callmen, Samuel Simonton, William Butterworth, William Davis, John McGill, John Shaw, Geo. V. Brower, Peter Dahlinger, William H. Ward.

ENGINE No. 3.—Located on Prospect street, near Ellison. Engine second size Amoskeag, purchased in 1881 and in fair condition. Four-wheel hose cart built by Silsby M'f'g Co., carries 700 feet of hose; in fair condition. Captain, Chris. Cubby; Engineer, Chas. Wiley; drivers, Leonard Hartley and Daniel Leonard; callmen, James Irwin, Thos. G. Murphy, Joseph Meller, James B. Haley, Morris Rossell, George Wassmer, Christian Mundrich, Rinard Sherlock.

ENGINE No. 4.—Located on Slater street, near Jersey street. Engine second size Clapp & Jones, purchased in 1883 and in good condition. Hose wagon built by Sowerbutt, in good condition, carries 700 feet of hose, two 3-gallon extinguishers. Captain, Patrick Sweeney; Engineer, Alex. Thoms; drivers, John Cluney and John J. Condon; callmen, John J. Canning, Robert Dunphy, William Marshall, James Cullerton, Hugh Kennedy, William Morrison, John Marshall, Jeremiah O'Toole.

ENGINE No. 5.—Located on Water street between Main and West street bridges. Engine second size Silsby, purchased in 1884, in good condition. Hose wagon built by Sowerbutt, in good condition, carries 700 feet of hose, two 3-gallon extinguishers. Captain, William Cook; Engineer, Frank Blakely; drivers, John Lair and William Stannard; callmen, Chas. Harrison, Frank Geroe, Jacob Snyder, Peter Bradley, Peter Howden, John Messenger, Henry Snyder, Thos. N. Hallowell.

ENGINE No. 6.—Located on Market street, near Straight. Engine second size Clapp & Jones, purchased in 1886 and in good condition. Hose wagon built by John Post, in good condition, carries 700 feet of hose, two 3-gallon extinguishers. Captain, Edward J. Coleman; Engineer, Frank Costello; drivers, Louis Haasser, James O'Neill; callmen, Thos. Checkley, Josiah Barton, John Frolich, James Thoms, Frank McLaughlin, John Hart, Edward Kirwin, Marinus Heintjes.

ENGINE No. 7.—Located at 298 Tyler street. Engine third size Clapp & Jones, purchased in 1876, in good condition. Hose wagon built by John Post, in good condition, carries 700 feet of hose, two 3-gallon extinguishers. Captain, William Allen; Engineer, William Farrell; drivers,

John W. Bowden, A. Perrins; callmen, David Devine, George Mills, Thos. Fish, Ben. Sanderson, Henry Harding, Joseph Rogers, William Butterworth, John Clark, W. B. Pohlman.

ENGINE No. 8.—Located on Wayne avenue, corner of Liberty street. Engine third size Silsby, purchased in 1890, in good condition. Hose wagon built by Post & Doremus, in good condition, carries 700 feet of hose, two 3-gallon extinguishers. Captain, William Boyle; Engineer, Thos. Donohue; drivers, John Ellis and Robert Wright; callmen, Adam Banghart, John Nagle, James Dunkerly, Jas. C. Matthews, Jr., John W. La Rue, Chris. Rafferty, Kerrin Keys, James McMullen.

ENGINE No. 9.—Located on Main street near Washington avenue. Engine third size Silsby, purchased in 1891, in good condition. Hose wagon in good condition, carries 700 feet of hose. Captain, Peter Riley; Engineer, Henry L. Reed; drivers, Michael Farrell and Allison Roswell; callmen, Nicholas R. Snyder, George Slater, John C. Garside, John O'Neil, Frank Rever, John Glass, Charles F. Saulter, Michael Berghorn.

TRUCK No. 1.—Located on Jackson street, near Green street. Truck built by Babcock Fire Extinguishing M'f'g Co., of Chicago, 1889, carries one 85-foot extension aerial ladder, one 55-foot extension ladder, one 38-foot, one 30-foot, one 25-foot, one 20-foot, one 14-foot, one 12-foot; two 3-gallon extinguishers, poles, hooks, ropes, etc. Captain, Joseph Kearney; Tillerman, Thomas Elvin; Extra Tillerman, Martin Brandt; driver, David McAllister; callmen,

James Jones, Thomas Fanning, Joseph Hutton, Richard Moore, Timothy Phalon, William J. Stewart, Edward Kilpatrick, Thomas Hardiman.

TRUCK NO. 2.—Located in Prospect street, near Ellison street. Truck built by Reading Fire Apparatus Co., 1881, carries one 65-foot extension, one 35-foot, two 30-foot, one 26-foot, one 19-foot, one 12-foot, one 9-foot and one 6-foot roof ladder; two 5-gallon extinguishers, poles, hooks, ropes, etc. Captain, John Weber; Tillermen, John Specht and John Vesey; driver, Richard Cubby; callmen, Gustave Specht, Charles Fahrenbach, Samuel Close, George Muth, Albert Merceir, Thomas Armstrong, Felix McCann, John Thomson.

TRUCK NO. 3.—Located corner of Auburn and Godwin streets. Truck built by E. V. Leverich, 1881, carries one 65-foot extension, one 38-foot, one 30-foot, one 26-foot, two 24-foot, one 18-foot, one 12-foot roof ladder; two 5-gallon extinguishers, poles, hooks, ropes, etc. Captain, Stewart Taylor; Tillermen, Nelson Norris and Harry Lister; driver, George Bunting; callmen, N. C. Quackenbush, James H. Coyle, William R. Close, John J. Hawley, George Carr, Christopher Murphy, H. M. Butler, Archie Irwin.

CHEMICAL NO. 1.—Located in Hotel street, near Market street. Engine, Babcock, double 60-gallon, with 400 feet of hose in two lines, purchased 1890, in good condition. Captain, William Campbell; Extr. Engineer, Michael Halnan; drivers, John Breen and Andrew Knaus.

HOSE HOUSE AND COAL DEPOT.— Located on Bridge

street, near Tyler street. One second size Nussey engine, in reserve, purchased in 1876, in good condition. One supply wagon for carrying coal, built by William Walker, in good condition.

Driver to chief engineer, George Pfitzenmayer; keeper hose house, George Slinguland; lineman to fire alarm, Joseph Chapman.

FIRE HOSE.—There are at present 11,200 feet of first-class, 1,500 feet of second class, and 1,100 feet of third-class hose in the department.

The number of signal boxes and instruments is as follows: 10-circuit repeater, 1; bell strikers, 5; engine house gongs, 15; engineers' gongs, 6; small tappers, 39; signal boxes, 102; galvanometers, 11; cut-offs, 9; indicators, 2; markers, 7. There are about 90 miles of wire in circuit.

LOCATION OF BELL STRIKERS.—Second Reformed church, corner Water and Temple streets; First Baptist church, corner Van Houten and Washington streets; First Presbyterian church, corner Ward and Main streets; No. 6 public school, corner Summer and Ellison streets; No. 8 engine house, corner Wayne avenue and Liberty street.

BATTERY.—The battery consists of 475 cells of gravity.

POLES, BRACKETS AND TRIPODS.—Fire alarm telegraph poles, 825; American Rapid and Western Union, 86; telephone and electric light, 250; tripods and brackets, 325.

E. S. Fields, Captain.   F. King, Captain.
C. Cubby, Captain.   P. Sweeney, Captain.

CHAPTER X.

THE BENEVOLENT ASSOCIATION.

Its Organization and Reorganization — Past and Present Officers — Its Beneficiary Features — Widows and Orphans — Rules and Regulations.

OCTOBER 20th, 1851, a meeting was held at No. 69 Main street (the store of First Assistant Chief Patrick Curran), for the purpose of organizing a benevolent association. The following-named gentlemen were present: From the Board of Engineers, Patrick Curran; from No. 1, William Sykes, Andrew Moser and Daniel Miller; from No. 3, Robert Miller, Thomas Bailey and William Fielding; from No. 5, Thomas Hindle, Lewis Simpson and William Douglas; from Hook and Ladder Co. No. 1, Horatio M. Lane, George English and John Bowering. Patrick Curran was elected chairman and Horatio M. Lane secretary. But little business was done except to authorize William Sykes to procure a constitution. November 11th another meeting was held, at which William Sykes presided. The proposed constitution was read, and the adjournment to Nov. 7th followed. Upon the last mentioned date a permanent organization was effected, and the following officers were elected: Patrick Curran, president; Thomas Hindle, vice-president; Horatio M. Lane, secretary; Andrew Moser,

THE BENEVOLENT ASSOCIATION.

treasurer. December 2d, 1851, a code of by-laws was adopted and the association was fairly launched. From that day to the present its career has been one of usefulness in the line of charitable work.

The association was reorganized May 20th, 1890, as the Firemen's Benevolent Association of the City of Paterson, N. J. Any sick or disabled fireman of the present department is entitled to the sum of $7.00 per week. Beneficiaries of the old volunteer department, of whom there are three, and members of the Exempt Association are entitled to the sum of $5.00 per week. Widows or orphans of beneficiaries of the old volunteer department or Exempt Association are entitled to the sum of $50 per annum. Widows or orphans of members of the present department are entitled to the sum of $100 per annum. Any beneficiary of this association may be stricken from the list at any time by a majority vote of the Board of Trustees.

The present officers of the association are: President, Wm. B. Campbell; Vice-President, Wm. Douglas; Secretary, Nat. C. Quackenbush; Treasurer, John McKiernan; Finance Committee, Thos. Whowell, Wm. Cook, Wm. Boyle.

Roll of Representatives: Chief Engineer John Stagg; Engine 1, Wm. Post, Joseph Backalan; Engine 2, John McGill, George Brower; Engine 3, Christopher Cubby, James Irwin; Engine 4, Jas. Cullerton, John J. Canning; Engine 5, Wm. Cook, Peter Bradley; Engine 6, Edward J. Coleman, Thos. Checkley; Engine 7, George Mills, David Devine; Engine 8, Wm. Boyle, Jas. McMullen; Engine 9,

Peter Riley, John Garside; Chemical 1, Wm. B. Campbell, Andrew Knaus; Truck 1, David McAllister, James Jones; Truck 2, Gustave Specht, Felix McCann; Truck 3, Wm. R. Close, Nat. C. Quackenbush; Exempt Association, Jno. McKiernan, Thos. Whowell.

Roll of Trustees: Engine 1, Daniel Gregory; Engine 2, Wm. Ward; Engine 3, Maurice Rozelle; Engine 4, John Marshall; Engine 5, Frank Geroe; Engine 6, Josiah Barton; Engine 7, Thos. Fish; Engine 8, Chris. J. Rafferty; Engine 9, John J. O'Neill; Chemical 1, John Breen; Truck 1, Joseph Hutton; Truck 2, George Muth; Truck 3, James H. Coyle; Exempt Association, Wm. Douglas.

Officers: Wm. Douglas, chairman; Nat. C. Quackenbush, secretary. Widows' Committee: C. J. Rafferty, M. Rozelle, J. H. Coyle, J. Barton, D. Gregory.

There are at present five firemen and the widows and orphans of twenty-six deceased firemen drawing relief from the association.

CHAPTER XI.

THE EXEMPT ASSOCIATION.

The Plan of Organization—Permanent Officers—Fair at Washington Hall—Installed in Its New House—Present Affairs of the Association—A Burial Clause Inserted in the By-Laws.

THE project of organizing an association of exempt firemen was talked of for many years before it became an accomplished fact. In November, 1882, the following notice appeared in the Paterson daily papers:

NOTICE.—To the Exempt Firemen of the City of Paterson, N. J.: You are requested to attend a meeting to be held on Monday evening, November 27th, 1882, at 8 o'clock, at the engine house of the Washington Steam Fire Engine Co., No. 3, for the purpose of forming an Exempt Firemen's Association. Signed: John W. Bensen, William Dobson, John McKiernan, William C. Martin, James I. King, Thomas Healey, Patrick Sweeney, Will Strong.

In response to this call ninety-six exempt firemen met at Engine 3's house. Ex-Chief John McKiernan called the meeting to order and was elected chairman. John Johnson, of Engine 4, was elected secretary. After considerable discussion regarding the plan of organization, a motion to make the society a beneficial one was lost and it was agreed to form a social association. Peter Fields, Bartholomew

Riley, Lambert Romaine, John W. Bensen and George W.
Pollitt were appointed a committee on permanent organization. They reported the following names for permanent
officers: John McKiernan, president; William C. Martin,
vice-president; John Johnson, secretary; John W. Bensen,
treasurer. A committee on by-laws was appointed, consisting of John W. Bensen, Geo. W. Pollitt, John MacDonald,
David I. Turnbull and James I. King. At the next meeting, February 7th, 1883, the committee on by-laws presented
their report, which was adopted. Garret Van Houten,
Geo. W. Pollitt, Charles M. King, John Sullivan and John
I. Spittel were elected the first board of trustees, and Joseph
Buckley, John C. McBride and Philip Chapman were
appointed as a standing committee. For a number of years
the association met quarterly at the several fire houses upon
invitation from the companies. The quarters of engines 1,
2, 3, 5 and 6, and truck No. 2 were made use of until 1888.
During the month of October, 1887, a fair was held at
Washington Hall, the proceeds netting $2,000. At the
annual meeting held in December, 1887, it was voted to
establish permanent headquarters, and Geo. W. Pollitt,
John W. Bensen and John I. Spittel were appointed a
committee to procure suitable rooms. At a special meeting
held at engine 3's house in January, 1888, the committee
reported in favor of leasing the rooms on the second floor
of the building No. 169 Market street. The report was
adopted and the same committee was authorized to expend
a sufficient amount to suitably decorate and furnish the
rooms. The rooms were informally opened Wednesday,

February 22d, 1888, and the association was comfortably installed in its new home, which was made use of until May 1st, 1892, when the association took possession of the frame building corner of Clark and Smith streets, lately purchased by them.

The association is in a first-class condition, has upwards of five hundred members and is receiving accessions constantly. The rooms comprise parlor, smoking and sitting room, kitchen and dining room on the first floor; front and rear parlor, game room, bath room, reading room and directors' room on second floor. The reading room is supplied with all the leading daily and weekly newspapers, magazines, etc., and the game room with various games, cards, dominos, chess, checkers, etc.

At a meeting held at engine 1's house, March 7th, 1883, twenty-two members signed a proposed plan for burial insurance, and at a meeting held at engine 2's house, July 11th, 1883, an organization was formed with the following officers: John McKiernan, president; William C. Martin, vice-president; Charles M. King, secretary; John W. Bensen, treasurer. Directors: Garret Van Houten, James I. King, John I. Spittel, Henry L. Reid and William Dobson. The assessment at a death was $1.10 per member. The membership increased to fifty-nine, and the fund existed until the Exempt Association adopted a burial clause in their by-laws.

The officers of the association are: President, John McKiernan; Vice-President, Daniel Gregory; Recording

Secretary, John I. Spittel; Financial Secretary, William Carey; Treasurer, Charles M. King.

Directors:. James Kearney, William Fielding, Thomas Whowell, William C. Martin, William Marshall, William Hobson.

Standing committees: John T. Pollitt, Samuel Holt, Henry Bush, Henry L. Reed.

CHAPTER XII.

BIOGRAPHICAL SKETCHES.

Some of the Officers of the Old and New Departments Who Have Made Fire History—Chief Stagg and His Staff—Exempt Veteran Firemen Whose Names Are Household Words.

JOHN STAGG, Chief of the Fire Department at Paterson, N. J., was born in that city December 16th, 1843. Mr. Stagg was educated in the public schools of his native city. In 1857 he went to work in the *Guardian* office and carried papers for about three years, working all day in the office and carrying papers evenings at a salary of $1.25 a week, but that was considered good pay in those days. He worked in the job department of the *Guardian* until 1862, when he enlisted in Company A, 11th New Jersey Volunteers. He served with the 11th Regiment as private, corporal, sergeant and quartermaster sergeant until, when before Petersburg in 1864, he was transferred to the First Michigan Cavalry, commanded by General Peter Stagg. He was at once promoted to second lieutenant and soon after to first lieutenant and aid-de-camp on his brother's staff, and served as such in the cavalry raid through the Shenandoah valley and around Richmond until the close of the war. The brigade was then ordered to

Utah on special service and shortly after, in April, 1866, was mustered out.

Mr. Stagg then drifted up into the gold mines in Montana and "roughed it" until September, 1868, when he returned to Paterson. He was immediately employed at his old place in the *Guardian* office and, pulling off his coat and rolling up his sleeves, went to work as if he had been there the day before, instead of having gone through four years of the most exciting sort of life, full of hair-breadth escapes in battle, skirmish and raid, two years of which were literally in the saddle. Afterwards he was business manager of the *Morning Call*, which he continued until appointed chief engineer of the present department, May 6th, 1891.

He joined Passaic Engine Co. No. 1 the same year he returned to Paterson (1868), and has been an active fireman ever since. He has always been foremost in everything appertaining to the department, rarely missing a fire in over twenty years. He served as secretary and foreman of his company, and was elected chief after one of the most stubborn and hotly contested campaigns ever known in Paterson. Chief Stagg is a member of the National Association of Fire Engineers, and takes a deep interest in the firemen's organizations of his state.

JAMES C. MILLS, First Assistant Engineer, was born in Paterson, N. J., in the year 1847, and is by occupation a silk throwster. At time of appointment in 1891 he was foreman in the silk mill of R. & H. Adams. He joined Protection Engine Co. No. 5 in January, 1871, and served with that company until the disbandment of the department, and then was appointed a callman. While in Engine No. 5 his comrades placed him in the following offices: Assistant foreman, foreman, vice-president and president. Chief Mills served in the late war in a New Jersey regiment and at the expiration of service received an honorable discharge.

JOHN GILLMORE was born in Girvin, Scotland, January 23, 1845, and on October 18th, 1865, he came to America and made his home in Paterson, where he has since lived. His occupation was that of a loom fixer, and he served as foreman and loom fixer for nineteen years in the large silk mill owned by Hamil & Booth. In 1871 he joined Engine Co. No. 6, and in 1880 he was elected foreman of this company and remained an active member until the reorganizing of the company from a volunteer to a paid company.

In 1890 he was elected by the board of aldermen to the office of assistant chief, and in the following year (1891) he was re-elected under the new law to hold the position of assistant chief on good behavior, which position he now holds.

WILLIAM B. CAMPBELL, President of the Firemen's Benevolent Association, was born in the Sixth Ward of Paterson in 1856; he is a machinist by trade, and his father was a fireman some thirty years ago, having been one of Washington No. 3's most active members in the "fifties." The subject of this sketch developed a fondness for running to fires when but a little urchin, and in common with his playmates in the sixth ward the tap of the fire bell was the signal which brought out every boy whose ears caught the sound. He became an active member of Neptune Engine Co. No. 2 on December 6th, 1876; since that time has been foremost in promoting the interests of his company. He has been honored by his company, having served them as assistant foreman, foreman and president. He holds the last-named position at the present time. He was elected a representative to the Benevolent Association in April, 1879, and has been re-elected annually since that time, serving on the relief committee for seven years. May, 1888, he was elected president of the Benevolent Association. Mr. Campbell has frequently represented his company in the annual convention of the fire department, and he is looked upon by all his associates and acquaintances as one who is a thorough fireman, with a love for the business that has made him a typical volunteer fireman. He is now captain of Chemical No. 1.

WILLIAM DOUGLAS, Vice-President of the Benevolent Association, was born in Paterson, August 19th, 1853. His father, William Douglas, was for many years an active member of Engine Co. No. 5, and served a term as assistant engineer. The subject of this sketch was a runner with and an ardent admirer of No. 5, and as soon as he had attained his majority (August 18, 1874), he became an active member and has ever since that time maintained a lively interest in the affairs and welfare of the company. He has been the recipient of many honors at the hands of his fellow members, having held every office within their gift except that of treasurer. In April, 1875, Mr. Douglas was elected a representative from No. 5 to the Benevolent Association and was at once elected vice-president. With the exception of one year (1883) when he was out of town he has been in the Benevolent board and has held every office except that of president and treasurer. The greater portion of the time he has been a member of the finance committee, often the chairman of it, and he is looked upon by his associates as one whose judgment is good and wise. Mr. Douglas has been in the employ of Messrs. R. & H. Adams (cotton and silk manufacturers) since 1870. The last fifteen years he has been the superintendent of the three mills of the Adams Bros. He has the confidence of his employers to the fullest extent, and he is in every way a credit to the department of which he is a member.

NATHANIEL C. QUACKENBUSH, secretary of the Benevolent Association, was born in Paterson October 4th, 1855. He became an active member of Cataract Hose Co., No. 2, July 7, 1879, having been a runner with that company for some time previous to his election. He was elected steward in the same month, and in December of the same year was elected secretary, which office he held for two years, when he was elected foreman. At the expiration of his term he was elected financial secretary for one year, when he was again chosen recording secretary, to which office he was re-elected from year to year until the company was disbanded in the month of March, 1889, having held a prominent office in his company for a period of nearly ten years. Mr. Quackenbush and one other were the originators of the idea of having a truck company to succeed Cataract Hose Co., whose house and apparatus were burned on the night of November 9, 1888. Mr Quackenbush was elected secretary of that company (which was known as Rapid H. & L. Co. No. 3) when it was organized, and has held that office until the present time, having been appointed call man when the department was changed to a paid system, February 28, 1890. He was assistant secretary of the Benevolent Association during the years 1881-'82, and secretary in the years 1883-'84. He was elected secretary of the Benevolent Association when it was re-organized, May 20, 1890, and has held the office till the present time; has also been a member of the finance committee, and at present is treasurer of the Call Men's Association. Mr. Quackenbush is a carpenter and builder and commissioner of public instruction representing the fifth ward, having been appointed as a Democrat by Mayor Beveridge, March 28, 1892, for a term of two years. Member of Exempt Association.

JOHN McKIERNAN, treasurer of the Benevolent Association, was born in Paterson, August 18, 1833. He became a member of Washington Engine Co. No. 3, in February, 1852, and was elected treasurer of his company in October, 1855, and was re-elected in 1856. In May, 1859, he was elected foreman and served until May, 1862, when he was elected assistant engineer of the Paterson Fire Department. In September, 1862, he went to the war as captain of Company A, 25th Regiment, New Jersey Volunteers, which company was composed mainly of members of Mr. McKiernan's fire company. He served as senior captain in all the engagements in which his regiment took part, and they were many, as his regiment has a record of which its surviving members may be proud.

Toward the close of the war Capt. McKiernan served in the Quartermaster's Department at Newbern, N. C. At the close of the rebellion he returned home with all the honors of a brave soldier. But more honors were in store for him. He was immediately elected foreman of his company, in which capacity he served until May, 1868, when he was elected chief engineer of the department. In 1857 he was elected treasurer of the Paterson Firemen's Benevolent Fund. In May, 1869, he was again elected treasurer of the Fund, and he has served in that capacity until the present time. In 1880 he was elected treasurer of the New Jersey State Firemen's Association, and he has been re-elected every term since. In November, 1882, at the organization of the Exempt Firemen's Association of Paterson, he was elected as its president, which office he also now holds. He is also president of the Exempt Firemen's Beneficial Association of his department. He has also been president of Washington Engine Co. No. 3 for the past fifteen years. Mr. McKiernan was among the organizers of the State Firemen's Association of New Jersey. He is very popular in the fire department, and has received all the honors the fire department can bestow. He has often been importuned by his friends to accept offices of a political nature, but has always declined. He is a member of the firm of Doremus & McKiernan, who have a large store and crockery warehouse on Main street.

ROBERT GLEDHILL, the genial vice-president of the Exempts, is a gentlemen so well known in this city that he does not need an extended notice here. Mr. Gledhill was in active service in the department from 1863 until 1878, when he took out his certificate. He is the youngest son of one of the oldest residents of Paterson, Mr. Joseph Gledhill, who came to this city in 1817. The subject of this sketch has enjoyed a long and prosperous business career, having started in the drug business in 1848, as clerk for R. T. Creamer, who was then located on the corner of Main and Van Houten streets. It was not long before he became proprietor, and shortly afterward he moved his store to Main street, and in 1878 sold out his interest to Mr. Kent. Since that time he has not been actively engaged in business, but has been more or less identified with any movement looking towards Paterson's commercial prosperity. He has filled the measure of his duties as a good citizen by serving four years as School Commissioner, and for two years he was elected representative from Passaic Steamer No. 1.

EX-CHIEF ANDREW MOSER. This gallant old fireman is the veteran of the Exempt Association, and was the oldest member of the volunteer department when it disbanded. He has a record that he can feel justly proud of. He joined Passaic Engine Company in October, 1847, and served continuously in that company forty-seven years. During all that time he failed to respond to roll-call after a fire only six times. Mr. Moser has never been sick a day in his life, and he is far more active to-day than many a man of half his age. During his service in No. 1 he held all the different offices in the gift of the company and was the president of the stock company from the time of its incorporation until it was mustered out. Mr. Moser was born in Alsace, France, and came to this country in the spring of 1832, and accepted a position in Holtzman's old cotton mill. He started in the confectionery business on his own account in 1842, and has been engaged in it until this spring when he retired. Mr. Moser is very popular among the younger members of the association, and his large experience makes him a widely sought authority on all matters of interest to firemen.

JOHN I. SPITTEL was born in the city of Paterson, January 4th, 1847. He joined the volunteer department in 1868, first becoming a member of Engine No. 2, and served in that company for several years, when he joined Engine No. 3, and remained with them until the starting of the paid department. During that time he held the office of vice-president for five years under President McKiernan, and was elected foreman of the company in 1881. When the association was organized he was chosen as one of the original board of directors and held that position until 1886, when he was elected secretary, and has been re-elected at every election since then.

EX-CHIEF JOHN F. MURPHY was born in this city in April, 1850. In 1867 he left his home here and went to Marquette, Mich., and remained there about three years. His first experiences as a volunteer fireman occurred while he was a resident of that city, and the knowledge he gained there proved useful to him afterward. He was in active service during the big fire in June, 1869, one of the largest

P. REILLY, Captain.   J. KEARNEY, Captain.
J. WEBER, Captain.   S. TAYLOR, Captain.

conflagrations in the West. Mr. Murphy came back to Paterson in July, 1870, and on his return he became a runner with engine No. 6, and three years later he joined the association connected with Passaic No. 1, and became an active member of the company in April, 1875, and remained with it until it disbanded. Shortly afterward he was elected assistant chief of the paid department, and on the resignation of Chief Turnbull he was appointed to fill the vacancy. He served acceptably until his term expired, when he was succeeded by John Stagg, the present chief.

MAJOR JAMES McKIERNAN was born in Paterson in 1828. He was one of the organizers of Jackson Fire Co., No. 4, and was assistant foreman and then foreman of the company. In 1861, when the civil war broke out, Major McKiernan was chief engineer of the Paterson Fire Department. He at once enlisted a company of one hundred men, nearly all firemen, and led them to Trenton. The boys elected him their captain and he was mustered in the United States service as captain of Company G, Seventh N. J. Volunteers. He served in the Army of the Potomac and was wounded and taken prisoner June 3d, 1862, at Fair Oaks. He was promoted to be major for gallant service. He served as commander of Farragut Post 28, of this city. He died December 26, 1882, universally lamented.

EX-CHIEF DAVID I. TURNBULL was one of the organizers of the Exempt Association. He was born in 1840 in Paterson, and always took a lively interest in the fire department from the time of joining Neptune Engine Co., No. 2, in 1863, until the disbandment of the volunteers.

His comrades in the company honored him by electing to the offices of president, secretary and treasurer for several terms, and as foreman two years. In the year 1877 he was elected by the firemen to serve as chief engineer for two years, and in 1889 was appointed to the same office by the board of aldermen. After serving one year he resigned the position. Most of his life has been spent in Rogers Locomotive Works as machinist and millwright. Chief Turnbull was one of the promoters of the State Firemen's Association, of which the Paterson Fire Department Benefit Fund is a branch.

CHAPTER XIII.

RULES AND REGULATIONS OF THE FIRE DEPARTMENT.

Fire Department Officials—Qualifications of Members—Pay of the Force—Badges and Uniforms—Insignia of Office—Fire Alarm Telegraph—Burial Fund Association.

RULES and regulations for the government of the fire department were adopted August 3, 1891, with these officials in office:

Mayor, Thomas Beveridge; committee on fire department, John Macdonald, *Chairman;* John Hartley, William R. Harding, James Miller, Joseph Keppler, *Clerk*, John T. Pollitt; chief engineer of fire department, John Stagg; assistant engineers, James C. Mills, John Gillmore; superintendent of fire alarm telegraph, James F. Zeluff; veterinary surgeon, Dr. William Herbert Lowe.

The rules and regulations are as follows: The fire department of the City of Paterson shall consist of a chief and two assistant engineers, superintendent of fire alarm telegraph, veterinary surgeon, captains, engineers, drivers and call men to act as stokers, hosemen, laddermen and other officers, members and employees, as the service may from time to time require, all of whom shall be under control of the board of aldermen and subject to rules and regulations of the department, and orders that may be issued by the chief engineer and approved by said board of aldermen or committee on fire department.

QUALIFICATIONS OF MEMBERSHIP.—Persons to be eligible to membership in the department must be residents of the City of Paterson, citizens of the United States, of good moral character, and able to read and write the English language understandingly. They shall be in good health, sound in body and mind, certified to by the city physician, that he is physically capable of performing the duties required of him, and not engaged in any business that will prevent them from instantly responding to an alarm.

Every officer or member before entering on his duties, shall sign an agreement, to be deposited with the chief engineer, that he will abide by and conform to all rules and regulations established by the committee and approved by the board of aldermen for the government of the department, and be subject to the penalties named therein.

Every member shall be furnished by the chief with a copy of the rules and regulations governing the department. All members of the permanent force shall give their entire time to the interest of the fire department, and no outside work will be permitted.

APPLICATIONS.—All applications for membership shall be made in the handwriting of the applicant, who shall present the same in person to the special committee on fire department or any regular committee on fire department who may have charge hereafter.

All applicants for the position of engineers of steamers

must stand a practical examination as to their abilities for looking after the same.

PAY OF THE FORCE.—The pay of the force is hereby fixed as follows, per annum: Chief engineer, $1,500; assistant engineers, $1,000; superintendent of fire alarm telegraph, $1,000; veterinary surgeon, $500; captains, $900; engineers, $875; drivers, $850; tillermen, $850; hosemen, laddermen and stokers at call, per annum, $150.

CHIEF ENGINEER.—The chief engineer shall have sole and entire command at fires and alarms of fire over all members of the department, and all apparatus and appurtenances belonging to the same, and direct all measures he may deem proper for the extinguishment of fires. He shall devote his whole time to the performance of the duties of his office. He shall visit each engine, truck and hose house weekly, or as often as possible, and report to the committee on fire department any suggestions for the improvement of the fire department he may deem necessary.

He shall cause all repairs and other work on account of fire department to be done, as far as possible, by members of the permanent force. He shall report to the committee company officers or members, if any there be, delinquent in the performance of their duties assigned them, and each month those absent from fire alarms, also members who have assigned their pay.

He may, from time to time, issue such orders for the government of the members as he may deem proper, subject to approval by fire committee.

He shall have power to suspend any officer or member

of the department for neglect of duty or disorderly conduct, said suspension to remain in force pending action of fire committee. He shall also have charge of hose and coal depot, and place a man on permanent duty there.

He shall not absent himself from the city without consent of majority of the fire committee.

ASSISTANT ENGINEERS.—In the absence of the chief engineer of the department, he shall designate the senior assistant engineer of the department to command and perform all the duties, assume all the responsibilities and functions of the chief of department, and perform such other duties as his superior may direct.

It shall be the duty of the assistant engineers: 1. Be on duty constantly, day and night, at their respective headquarters, except when called elsewhere on department business, or on leave of absence. 2. They shall attend all fires at stations to which they may be assigned, detailed or called, and report promptly their arrival to the officer in command. 3. The first to arrive at a fire to assume command and have full control until command is assumed by the chief engineer of the department. 4. Direct the movement of officers and men under their command, and extinguish the fires with the least possible loss by fire and water. 5. Cause all companies not needed to promptly return to quarters. 6. In case of fire, promptly report any dangerous buildings to the chief engineer of department. 7. Perform such other duties as their superior may direct.

SUPERINTENDENT OF FIRE ALARM TELEGRAPH. — The Superintendent of Fire Alarm Telegraph shall have entire charge and control of the fire alarm telegraph, subject to such rules and regulations as may be made from time to time by the committee. He shall at all times have the telegraph apparatus in perfect order, and any neglect so to do shall be deemed cause for dismissal.

He shall promptly report to the chief engineer any interruption in the working of the lines or apparatus whereby there shall be a delay in giving or receiving an alarm of fire, unless the same is immediately repaired.

In such report he shall state what amount of delay will occur in repairing the same, and when repaired he shall see that the chief engineer has notice of the fact.

LINEMAN.—The Fire Alarm Telegraph Lineman shall be under the supervision of the superintendent of fire alarm telegraph.

VETERINARY SURGEON.—The Veterinary Surgeon shall have, under the direction of the committee, general charge and direction as to the care and management of the horses belonging to the department, giving such surgical and medical care as may be required.

All orders pertaining to the shoeing of horses in the department, and any cause removing the horses from active duty, shall be made through the office and with the consent of the chief engineer.

He shall give his opinion as to all horses about to be purchased, and make such examinations as may be required by the committee.

CAPTAINS.—Captains of companies shall have command

and control of their companies, and all members shall obey their orders implicitly.

They shall see that the apparatus in their care, and the building in which the same is deposited, and all articles in or belonging to the same, are kept clean and in order for immediate use.

They shall preserve order and discipline at all times in their respective companies and enforce a strict compliance with the rules and regulations of the department and the orders of the chief engineer. The Captains, on leaving quarters, shall designate who shall act until their return unless otherwise ordered.

They shall keep an accurate record of the membership of their respective companies, an account of all property entrusted to their care, and all absence from fires or neglect of duty on the part of the men of their command, in a book provided for that purpose, which record shall be open for inspection by the chief and assistant chief engineers, and members of their companies. They shall present a copy of same to the board of aldermen, through the chief engineer, on the first day of each month.

The Captains shall give their entire time to the interest of the fire department, and they shall at all times be in attendance at their quarters.

Any company receiving a still alarm of fire shall report the same to the chief engineer.

The Captain first arriving at a fire shall exercise command until the arrival of his superior officer.

ENGINEERS.—It shall be the duty of the engineer of each

steamer to give his entire time to the interest of the fire department, and he shall at all times be in attendance at his engine house.

He shall be held personally responsible for the care of the engine and heater. He shall accompany the engine to all fires and alarms of fire, and shall have full charge of the running of the engine, subject to the orders of the captain and all superior officers.

He shall see that at all times his engine is ready for use. Should an alarm of fire occur during the absence of either of the drivers, he must drive in his stead. He must also assist in the care of the house.

He shall do all repairs, if possible, when so ordered by his superior officers.

STOKERS.—The stoker may be assigned to that position from among the call men by the captain, and shall, under the direction of the engineer, assist in the care and management of the engine at fires.

They shall see that the engine is properly supplied with fuel, and perform such other duties as may be required of them by the engineer.

DRIVERS.—It shall be the duty of the drivers of each engine, hose wagon and hook and ladder truck to be in constant attendance at their respective houses. They shall have charge of the horses, harness and stables, &c., and have them well cleaned each morning.

They shall take charge of the horses of the company during the service of their apparatus at fires.

In cold and stormy weather, on arriving at a fire, they

shall blanket their horses, and if apparatus is placed in service, the driver will try and get shelter for their horses in the neighborhood.

When the horses return to the house wet by perspiration or stormy weather, they shall have them well cleaned, rubbed down and examined and ready for use.

It shall be the duty of the drivers to exercise their horses one hour daily (excepting Sunday and stormy weather), and at no time at exercise take them more than two blocks away from their respective houses.

They shall practice their horses at the 9.15 p. m. stroke of the alarm gong each night in going to their places in front of the apparatus, and they must snap the collar, and shall at each fire alarm from stations at which they do not answer first alarms, hitch their horses to their apparatus and remain hooked for the space of fifteen minutes, unless back tap is sooner received.

The drivers of hose wagons shall have charge of their respective apparatus, keep them clean and ready for service at all times, and also of the hose belonging thereto. He shall assist in the duties of the stable, and shall also assist in the care of the house. In exercising his horse he shall do so at a time when steamer horses are in the house, as at no time of exercising shall horses of steamer and hose wagon be out at the same time.

The drivers of engine, truck and hose wagon shall in no case after their respective companies have been relieved from duty at fires, run over any hose upon their return to their quarters.

Drivers of apparatus, while responding to an alarm of fire are forbidden to turn corners, or in and out of car tracks, faster than at a moderate trot, and drivers must give an alarm signal on their gong when approaching corners and crossings.

Racing to or from fires is strictly prohibited, and if the apparatus of several companies proceeds in the same street they shall do so in single file.

Drivers must at all times in going to a fire understand that direct orders from the chief or assistant engineers to quicken their pace must be obeyed.

TILLERMEN AND EXTRA TILLERMEN.—It shall be the duty of the tillermen of each truck to give their entire time to the interest of the fire department. And they shall be in constant attendance at their respective houses, accompanying their apparatus to all fires and alarms of fires, and assist the members of the companies in the performance of their duties at the fire. They shall take charge of and keep in neat and clean order their respective apparatus and house, and shall attend to keeping the beds and bunk room in order.

CALL HOSEMEN AND LADDERMEN.—The call men of the several companies shall, upon an alarm of fire from the section of the city to which they are assigned to duty, proceed promptly to the place of the fire, and perform any duty that may be required of them. They shall remain on duty until relieved by order, which shall be given only by the officer in command.

They shall, while on duty at fires, wear the regulation fire hat.

Any call man wishing to absent himself from the city, shall apply to the captain of his company, and the application shall be forwarded to the chief engineer for action, and under no circumstances shall there be more than two call men absent at one time from any one company.

Badges.—All members of the department shall be provided with badges, which shall be worn during the whole time when they shall be on duty.

Uniforms.—The captains, engineers, drivers and tillermen shall be required to keep their uniforms in a neat condition, and shall wear them at all times, except when permission is granted otherwise.

The uniforms of the permanent members of the department shall consist as follows:

Fire Hat.—For chief of department a white leather hat, having a gilded front pending from a gilt eagle's head, and attached to the front of his hat with the insignia of his rank painted upon it in black letters, shaded with red, and above the word "chief" in black letters shaded with red, upon a scroll of gold as per pattern.

For assistant chief of department, same as for the chief, with the insignia of his rank below the words "assistant chief."

For officers of engine companies, same as for the chief of department, except that it will be of black leather, and have a white patent leather stitched front, with the number of the company cut out of it near the bottom in plain block figures, on a background of black patent leather (three and one-half inches long, if it be a single figure, and two and one-half inches long, if it be a double figure), and with the insignia of rank above it in gold, shaded with red.

For officers of hook and ladder companies, same as for officers of engine companies, except that number of the company will be on a background of red patent leather.

For all other members of companies, same as for officers of engine companies, omitting the insignia of rank, and except that the front will be of black patent leather, with the number of the company on a background of white patent leather.

For all members of hook and ladder companies, same as for officers of hook and ladder companies, omitting the insignia of rank, and except that the front will be of red patent leather with the number of the company on a background of white patent leather, and the registered number of each member in white figures, one inch long, painted on a line below.

FATIGUE CAPS.—For the chief of department, of U. S. navy pattern, made of dark blue cloth, pure indigo dye, with band one and one-half inches, and quarters one and three-quarter inches high, stiffened with hair cloth sewed in the seam of top, and quarters to have small holes in the side for ventilation, and to be lined with red silk. A narrow welt around bottom of band and top seam of cap; the inner band to be of strong, serviceable leather, the visor to be plain black, solid patent leather, two inches wide, with rounded corners; the chin-strap of black patent leather, one-half inch wide, with slides of the same material fastened to each side of the cap with a small regulation button. The insignia of rank as prescribed to be placed on the quarters in the center of the front. the lower points resting nearly upon the upper edge of band.

For assistant chief of department and company officers, the same as for the chief of department., except the insignia of rank, which will be prescribed for them respectively.

For all other members, same as for company officers, omitting the insignia of rank, and substituting therefore a white metal Maltese cross, two inches square, with the letters "P. F. D." on the lower arm, a hook and ladder crossed on the right arm, a hydrant on the left arm, and with the registered number of each member in figures. three-eights of one inch long, in a circle one inch in diameter. to be fastened to the cap with an eye under each side arm, the lower arm resting on the upper edge of band.

COAT.—For the Chief of Department a double-breasted. close-fitting sack coat, made of dark blue cloth, pure indigo dye, cut to button close to the neck, rolling collar, and to reach to a point midway between the hip joint and the bend of the knee; to have eight medium-sized regulation buttons on each breast. grouped in pairs; the cuffs to be made to fit the wrists, and to be closed with three small regulation buttons; to have a pocket on the inside of each breast; the sleeves to be cut so as to be conveniently worn inside an overcoat; the coat to be lined with blue flannel and the sleeves with linen.

The prescribed insignia of rank to be placed on the end of the collar on each side.

For assistant chief of department same as for chief of department, except that buttons shall be placed equi-distant and the insignia of rank will be prescribed for them respectively.

For company officers, same as for the chief of department except that the buttons will be seven in number on each breast, placed equi-distant, and that the insignia of rank will be as prescribed for them respectively.

For all other members same as for company officers, except that it will be single-breasted and have six buttons.

For summer wear a coat may be worn of dark blue flannel, indigo dye, and in all other respects as above prescribed for the various grades, but without lining.

OVERCOAT.—For Chief of Department a double-breasted frock coat, with rolling collar, made according to pattern at headquarters, with lap seams, of best dark blue pilot cloth, pure indigo dye, in length to reach to the knee; to button up close to the neck, with eight large regulation buttons on each breast, grouped in pairs; three on each skirt behind and three of small size on each sleeve at the cuff; the skirt to be open behind; no outside pockets, but one inside on each breast; the skirts and back to be lined with flannel; the sleeves to be lined with linen and fit snugly at the wrists.

For all other officers and members, the same as for the chief of department, except that there shall be five regulation buttons on each breast, placed equi-distant.

VEST.—For all officers and members a single-breasted

vest, made of same material as the coat, without collar, and to button with five small regulation buttons to within five inches of the neck band.

For summer wear a vest may be worn of light cloth or flannel, dark blue indigo dye, and in all other respects as above prescribed.

TROWSERS.—For all officers and members to be made of the same material as the coat, with lap seams, to be cut to fit close around the waist, but loosely around the hams and legs, to admit of their free use. For summer or winter wear, trowsers may be made of heavier or lighter material of the same color and dye and in the manner prescribed.

SHIRTS.—For all officers to be of white linen or cotton, with white collar.

For all other members to be of dark blue flannel, double-breasted, with large rolling collar.

CRAVAT.—For all officers a black necktie or bow.

For all other members, of black silk to pass once around the neck, with flat knot in front.

INSIGNIA OF OFFICE.—For Chief of Department five trumpets measuring one and five sixteenths inches each, crossed with bell outward and projecting beyond mouthpiece so as to form a design one and one-half inches in diameter, to be embroidered in gold upon a circle of dark blue cloth.

For Assistant Chief of Department same as for the chief of department, except that there shall be three trumpets measuring one and one-half inches each, crossed with bells downward.

N. C. Quackenbush.

W. Campbell, Captain.

John McKiernan, Ex-Chief.

For Captains of engine companies there shall be two trumpets. The trumpets shall be parallel, with bell downwards, and close together, all on an oval of white metal or nickel plate. For captains of hook and ladder companies, two axes.

The insignia for the cap is to have the number of the company midway between the trumpets or axes.

COAT BADGE.—Same as for the cap, except that it shall be fastened with a pin and catch.

BUTTONS. — For Chief and Assistant Chiefs to be of white metal with gilt face, of the following description: For overcoat (except the cuff) to be round, one inch in diameter, with convex roughened face, having the initials " F. D." in block letters one-quarter of an inch high in the center.

For coat (except the cuffs) same as for overcoat except that it is to be three-quarters of one inch in diameter, having the initials " F. D." in block letters in the center, word " Paterson " on top and " City " on bottom.

For vests, cuffs of coat, and fatigue cap, same as for coat, except it be five-sixteenths of one inch in diameter.

For company officers and all other members, same as for chief of department, except that the buttons are to be of white metal throughout.

The uniforms of the members of the department shall be kept neat and clean at all times, and all uniforms shall be inspected by the chief, who may condemn any parts he may consider unfit for service, the same to be renewed within a reasonable time.

7

BURIAL FUND ASSOCIATION.—Was organized and by-laws adopted August 1st, 1892, with the object of providing a fund for the burial of the deceased members of the association.

The fund consists of an amount of money equal to the number of members, at the rate of one dollar per man.

Upon the death of a brother member in good standing, the sum of one hundred dollars shall be paid to his widow or nearest of kin.

HISTORY

OF

Paterson's Police Protection

THE EARLY METHODS THAT PREVAILED A QUARTER OF A CENTURY AGO — CONSTABLES: ONE ELECTED FOR EACH WARD — SPECIAL POLICE APPOINTED FOR STATED PERIODS.

A CITY MARSHAL THE ONLY SALARIED OFFICER.

A POLICE FORCE OF TEN MEN ORGANIZED — A FIXED SALARY OF FIVE HUNDRED DOLLARS PER ANNUM.

THE PRESENT POLICE DEPARTMENT.

ITS HISTORY AND ORGANIZATION UP TO DATE.

CHAPTER XIV.

ORGANIZATION OF THE POLICE FORCE.

A Record of Police Protection Written by Chief Graul—Some Exciting and Interesting Episodes Officially Related—The Force Up to Date.

THE writer is indebted to Chief Graul for the following condensed sketch of the Police Department:

Up to July 16th, 1866, Paterson had no police force other than the constables elected, one in each ward. The city then contained five wards: the North, East, West, South and Fifth wards. A city marshal was the only salaried police official who had been appointed by the mayor and aldermen up to that time, except special police who were appointed several years previous to the organization of the force, and who were hired by the city for stated evenings of the week to patrol Main street to prevent corner lounging and disorder; their tour of such duty being generally from seven to ten o'clock. Some of the constables were also employed in this duty. Many burglaries of private houses had been perpetrated on the outskirts of the city, and a great deal of valuable household goods carried off by the thieves, who appeared to come from outside of the city. These burglaries were carried on for some time. They became so frequent and extensive that the citizens got alarmed, and the mayor and aldermen, prompted by this fact, decided to organize a police force of ten men. That was consummated on July 16th, 1866, and the men so appointed were ordered to go on active duty August 1st following, with a fixed salary of $500 per annum.

Wm. G. Watson was mayor of the city, and the following constituted the board of aldermen:

James Bush and Charles P. Gurner, from the North ward.

John Reynolds and Halmagh Van Winkle, from the East ward.

Peter Simonton and Samuel Dean, from the West ward.

John Bowering and Wm. Atchinson, from the Fifth ward.

Joseph Stansfield and Wm. Killen, from the South ward.

Peter Dobbs was city marshal and head of the police department.

The men appointed on the force were as follows:

Benjamin Harris and Patrick Kenney, from the North ward.

Frederick G. Graul and John P. Conklin, from the East ward.

Henry E. Jones and Bernard Carrol, from the West ward.

John M. Kemp and John R. Spittle, from the Fifth ward.

George Dean and Edward Dunn, from the South ward.

They were distributed throughout the city in the night time, and Patrolmen Graul and Jones were detailed by the marshal to patrol the outskirts of the East ward, that being the location where all the burglaries had been committed. On the night of the 3d of August, the third night of duty, at about midnight, these two officers discovered the burglars prowling around the house of D. B. Grant, situated on the corner of East 18th street and Broadway. The burglars discovered the presence of the officers and endeavored to make their escape. They were captured, however, and proved to be the thieves who had committed all the burglaries in this neighborhood, a large amount of the stolen property being recovered by the officers from the residences of both burglars. They were tried on a number of indictments in this and Bergen county, were convicted and sent to Trenton State Prison for twenty-seven years each. The names of these burglars were Gustave Dorflinger and Peter Reinhardt. Dorflinger lived on Second Ave., New York City, and Reinhardt lived in a house situated in the woods back of Fort Lee, Bergen County. The latter place appeared to have been the headquarters of the thieves, as the greater amount of the plunder was found there. They travelled with horse and wagon, the horse being a fast roadster, and they generally cleaned out the parlors of houses; in some cases they took up carpets. Dorflinger was a native of Switzerland, and a very large and powerfully built man. He was very desperate, and carried a five-chamber Smith & Wesson revolver. When they discovered the presence of the officers on the night of the arrest, Reinhardt endeavored to make his escape by running down Broadway, toward the city. Patrolman Graul gave chase and captured him after a short run. Dorflinger stood his ground and Patrolman Jones took him into custody. Graul brought his prisoner back toward Jones and Dorflinger, and when within about 100 feet of where they were standing, Jones left his prisoner and came to handcuff Reinhardt, who was in Graul's custody. Just then Dorflinger started and ran out Broadway, toward the country. Graul said to Jones: "There goes your man." Jones replied: "Go and catch him." Graul gave chase and run Dorflinger down. Just as he did so, Dorflinger turned and fired his revolver at Graul. Graul grappled with the burglar, and a fierce struggle ensued, during which the burglar discharged his revolver again. Graul, having no weapon except a small club, fought to get possession of the burglar's revolver, which he succeeded in doing after a hard struggle. When the burglar saw he was losing ground in the struggle, and having lost possession of his murderous weapon, he broke loose from his captor and ran into the bushes, which were very thick on both sides of the road. Graul ordered him to stop, and upon his failing to do so, fired two shots at him, one of which took effect in the muscle of his right arm. Dorflinger concealed himself in the bushes, and could not be found that night, but was arrested two days later in New York city. Search was made for their horse and wagon, after Reinhardt had been brought to the lockup, and it was found concealed in the Van Buren woods on Broadway hill.

No more burglaries were committed after the capture of these two men, and citizens residing in the suburban parts of the city felt comparatively safe at night thereafter.

WILLIAM RYAN.
PRESIDENT BOARD OF POLICE COMMISSIONERS.

JAMES C. SIGLAR.
POLICE COMMISSIONER.

John R. Spittle, who had been appointed from the Fifth ward, declined to serve, and John P. Conklin, who had been appointed from the East ward, only served six days, and resigned Aug. 6th, 1866, and Thomas Maher was appointed to fill this vacancy. Maher only served two days. On the third day he came on duty in a very drunken condition, and Marshall Dobbs relieved him of his badge.

Aug. 20, 1866, Thomas Maher was dimissed, and Alexander Davison and Patrick Delaney were appointed. Oct. 1, 1866, the salaries of patrolmen were raised to $700 per annum. Jan. 7, 1867, Patrick Kenny resigned, and Daniel Gerve and Alexander W. Morgan were appointed. Feb. 18, 1867, Henry E. Jones resigned, and Patrick Cronin was appointed. Feb. 19, 1867, Fred'k G. Graul was appointed temporary roundsman by Marshal Dobbs. April 15, 1867, Cornelius Quackenbush was appointed city marshal, and Patrick Cronin and Patrick Delaney were dismissed. May 20, 1867, Fred'k G. Graul was appointed permanent roundsman, and John B. Rice and Anthony Ellison were appointed on the force. July 1, 1867, Bernard Carroll resigned (under charges). Aug. 5, 1867, Charles Simonton was appointed to the force. Oct. 7, 1867, John Parmley was appointed to the force. Oct. 21, 1867, Edward Dunn resigned, and Michael Keeff was appointed. Nov. 18, 1867, James Hewitt, Thomas Morrison, John Jordan and James Clark were appointed. Jan. 6, 1868, Anthony Ellison resigned, under charges, and Isaac Allman was appointed. Feb. 13, 1868, Benjamin Harris died. Feb. 17, 1868, John M. Kemp resigned, under charges, and Dewit C. Simonton was appointed. June 1, 1868, Alexander W. Morgan was appointed captain of police, but no duties were defined for the captain. July 9, 1868, Henry Barclay was appointed on the force. Aug. 31, 1868, John Parmley died. May 10, 1869, Matthias Vreeland, Jacob Huff, and James Condron were appointed. May 24, 1869, Adam Hargreaves, John Rooney, and John Keirwin were appointed. Aug. 3, 1869, Roundsman Graul's salary was increased to $800 per annum. Aug. 30, 1869, Isaac Allman resigned. Sept. 13, 1869, William Murray was appointed. Jan. 20, 1870, Capt. Morgan petitioned the board of aldermen to define his duties as captain of police. It was referred to the committee on police. March 14, 1870, the committee on police reported to the board on the matter referred to them in reference to defining the duties of the captain of police, and they recommend that the office of captain be abolished. The recommendation of the committee on police was adopted. March 28, 1870, John B. Rice was appointed second roundsman. June 13, 1870, Charles Holloway, Stephen Westervelt, William Duff, Patrick Guilfoil, William Roe, and John McBride were appointed. Sept. 12, 1870, the rank of roundsman was changed to sergeant, and Henry Barclay was appointed third sergeant. Oct. 12, 1870, the first station house was built, on the present site. Jan. 15, 1872, William Duff was dismissed. March 4, 1872, William Roe resigned. May 6, 1872, John B. Rice was appointed chief of police, under the new city charter, which did away with the office of city marshal; Michael Keeff was appointed sergeant to fill the vacancy caused by the promotion of Sergeant Rice to chief of police; William Wilds was appointed, and Jacob Huff resigned. June 3, 1872, Henry Rose, John Cronk, Martin R. Drew, Daniel McClory, John Wirzer, and John Binson were appointed. June 17, 1872, Alexander F. Anderson, Wm. Beatty, John Quinlan, Albert Polhamus, John Baxter, Joseph T. Brown, and Wm. Cairns were appointed. June 3, 1872, James Hewitt was appointed fourth sergeant. Aug. 5, 1872, John McBride was appointed fifth sergeant, and George Dean was dismissed. Oct 21, 1872, Alexander W. Morgan resigned. Jan. 20, 1873, Alexander F. Anderson and Dewitt C. Simonton resigned. April 7, 1873, Sergeant Graul was promoted to captain of police. May 19, 1873, John Keirwan was dismissed. Aug. 18, 1873, James Clark was dismissed. July 6, 1874, Wm. Cairns resigned. Jan. 4, 1875, Joseph T. Brown died. Oct. 4, 1875, Alexander Davidson resigned. Feb. 14, 1876, Chief of Police John B. Rice was dismissed, and Captain Graul was placed in charge of the department by the mayor. April 3, 1876, Captain Graul was promoted to chief of police by the unanimous vote of the board of aldermen. Dec. 4, 1876, James C. Watson resigned. Aug. 4, 1879, Charles Simonton was dismissed. April 19, 1880, John Baxter resigned. May 17, 1880, Isaac Harris, Charles Magee, John Powers, James Steel, Richard Mallinson, Wm. Bailey, Wm. Roe, Frank Becker, Wm. O'Rourke, James Dougherty, John Riker, Fred'k Bott, James McNamara, Thomas McInerney, Thomas Mullen, and Michael Phalon were appointed. June 21, 1880, John W. McCrea, John Dervel, Herman Hillman,

John Sommers, and Wm. Keys were appointed. July 11, 1880, Wm. Murray was dismissed. April 25, 1881, John Bimson was appointed captain of police. June 6, 1881, Wm. Bailey resigned. June 20, 1881, Wm. McCloud and Wm. Van Voorheis were appointed. May 15, 1882, John W. McCrea was dismissed. May 1, 1882, Herman Hillman resigned. July 11, 1882, David Kissich, Albert Magee, Wm. Mills, jr., Jacob Struck, John Fields, Charles Schocklin, Benajak W. Beardsley, Wm. Bland, John Holland, Mathew McGirr, and Miles W. Fitzgerald were appointed. April 24, 1883, Wm. Miles, jr., resigned. Oct. 15, 1883, Wm. McCloud was dismissed. Nov. 2, 1883, John Quinlan resigned (under charges). March 3, 1884, Henry Rose resigned (under charges). May 2, 1884, Charles Holloway died. Aug. 2, 1884, William Van Voorheis resigned. Nov. 17, 1885, James Dougherty was dismissed. April 11, 1885, James Steel resigned. April 5, 1886, John Dowd was dismissed. June 1, 1886, Wm. C. Rourke died. July 1, 1886, Peter Murphy, John W. Bradley, David Gibson, Thomas Walker, Patrick Kilt, Michael F. Bradley, Frank Bullock, Henry Vanderhoof, Patrick Fitzpatrick, John Rosenburgh, Charles W. Bush, James Evers, Peter Zeluff, Andrew Vreeland, Andrew J. McBride, John H. O'Hara, Charles F. Hoffman, John F. Bradley, Krine Overbeck, John McKelvey, Alexander Masterton, John Parkinsen, George W. Halstead, William Sweeney, John Romary, John Taylor, James Mullen, John Costello and Frank Whitla were appointed. July 12, 1886, Adam Hargreaves was appointed sergeant; Richard Wallinson was dismissed.

March 21, 1887, William Keys resigned (under charges). July 26, John H. O'Hara resigned (under charges). Aug. 1, Ed. Nolen, Frank Zimmer, Howard Gull, George T. Cazar, Samuel Kelly, William H. Adams and Charles Titus were appointed. May 7, 1888, Mathew McGirr and John Riker were appointed sergeants. Nov. 19, 1888, Wm. Sweeney was dismissed. Jan 15, 1889, John F. Bradley died. Jan. 8, 1890, Frederick Bott died. Feb. 26, 1890, James Condron died. April 26, 1890, George T. Cazar died. July 26, 1890, Mathias Vreeland died. May 18, 1891, Samuel Kelly was dismissed. June 15, 1891, John D. Garrison, Wm. H. Lord, Henry O'Brien, George Cox, Adolph Keppler, Nelson Graham, Daniel Dermond, Charles Robinson, John Draper, John H. Hurd, James Miller, John Stewart, Wm. E. Perry, John Fielding and John Campbell were appointed. Oct. 19, 1891, Daniel McClory resigned. Nov. 10, 1891, Wm. Beatty died. Nov. 16, 1891, Charles Boyle was appointed. Dec. 21, 1891, Thomas J. McGrath was appointed. Feb. 9, 1892, Michael Phalon died. Feb. 15, 1892, James Dougherty, Henry Titus, James Kehoe and Frank Sweetman were appointed. April 15, 1892, John Rosenberg was dismissed. May 9, 1892, John McKelvey resigned. May 26, 1892, Patrick Guilford was dismissed. Aug. 26, 1892, Alexander Master dismissed. Dec. 1, 1892, George Cox resigned under charges. March 10, 1892, The patrol wagon for this department arrived at this date. It had been ordered by the board of aldermen about one month before. March 18, 1892, the patrol wagon went into service. March 24, 1892, the mayor and new police justice met and appointed the new police commission. The mayor appointed James Johnson for two years and John MacDonald for one year. Justice Van Cleve appointed Wm. Ryan for two years and James C. Siglar for one year. March 28, 1892, the board of police commissioners organized; Commissioner Ryan was elected president and John F. Lee appointed clerk. One of the first acts of the board of police commissioners was to provide a stable adjoining the police station, where the patrol wagon, ambulance and police horse and vehicle could be kept; they also appointed two ambulance drivers, one for night service and one for day service, thus enabling the department to give prompt and better service.

CHAPTER XV.

THE AMENDED CHARTER.

An Oath of Affirmation—The Mayor to Appoint All Policemen, Subject to the Confirmation of the Board of Aldermen—A Chief of Police—A Day and Night Police Force—Their Duties and Compensation—Chief, Captain, Sergeants and Patrolmen—Uniform and Badges—Salary.

THE Amended Charter, approved March 23d, 1871, made it obligatory on every constable, before entering upon the duties of his office, to take and subscribe before the city clerk an oath of affirmation in the form prescribed for constables of townships, using the word "city" instead of "township;" and every constable, before entering on the duties of his office, should enter into bonds to the mayor and aldermen of the city, with one or more sureties to be approved by the board of aldermen, in such sum as might be fixed by ordinance from time to time.

Section 32 of the amended charter reads as follows:

"That the mayor shall appoint all policemen for said city, subject to the confirmation of the board of aldermen, and he shall have power to suspend any policeman, but shall, immediately upon so doing, communicate the fact of such suspension, with the reasons therefor, to the said board; and no policeman appointed and confirmed as aforesaid shall be removed except for cause and by the votes of a majority of all the members of said board. The mayor shall appoint one person from among the police force of said city, in May next after the passage of this act, to be chief of police, subject to the confirmation of said board, who shall perform the same duties as other policemen, and such additional duties as the board of aldermen shall by ordinance require of him; and the said chief of police shall hold such office during good behavior, unless sooner removed by a two-thirds vote of all the members of said board.

"Section 33: That in all actions now pending or to be brought hereafter before the recorder of said city, and in all proceedings in any of the criminal courts of the county of Passaic, the police officers of said city shall possess the same powers, perform the same duties and receive the same compensation as constables of the county of Passaic in like cases, except that no such officer shall receive any compensation for services under proceedings before said recorder."

An ordinance to establish, regulate and control a day and night police: to regulate and define the manner of their appointment and removal, their duties and compensation, was passed April 9th, 1875, of which the following is an abstract:

The police department shall consist of the chief of police, one captain and as many sergeants and patrolmen as the board of aldermen may from time to time appoint.

That during the illness or absence of the chief of police the captain of police shall execute and discharge the duties

JAS. JOHNSTON,
POLICE COMMISSIONER.

JOHN McDONALD,
POLICE COMMISSIONER.

of the office of chief of police, and at all other times shall discharge such duties as may be prescribed.

The members, when on duty, shall wear such uniform and badges, or signs of office, as shall from time to time be prescribed by the board of aldermen.

The annual salary of the captain of police shall be $950; of each sergeant, $900; of each patrolman, $850; and neither of said officers shall receive any other costs, fees or charges for services performed while on their regular duty.

Applications for appointment shall be made to the mayor in writing, and signed by the party by and for whom the application is made.

A certificate signed by a majority of the examining board (chief, city physician and committee on police), recommending any candidate presenting himself for such examination, shall be considered and taken by the mayor as sufficient evidence of such examination.

Each of the several ward constables shall be a police constable, and entitled to receive the fees upon the service of processes by them for violation of any of the laws or ordinances of the city, as full remuneration for the duties of their position of police constables.

In addition to such ward constables there shall be appointed by the board of aldermen such other police constables as they shall from time to time think necessary for the better government of the city, who shall receive as full remuneration for performing the duties of the position of police constable.

Any member of the police force may be expelled from

office by a majority vote of the board of aldermen, in addition to any other punishment to which he may be subject by law, against whom any of the following charges may be substantiated, namely: Intoxication; willful disobedience of orders; violent, coarse or insolent behavior to a superior in office, or any other person; receiving money or other valuable thing contrary to the statutes of the state, the ordinances of the city, or the rules and regulations of the police department; willful non-compliance with the said rules and regulations; inefficiency or gross neglect of duty; willfully maltreating, or doing unnecessary violence towards a prisoner or citizen, and such other causes as may be specially provided for or mentioned in said rules and regulations.

An act approved March 4th, 1880, enacted that "in all cases where any fireman or policeman of any incorporated city or town of this state is disabled while in the discharge of his public duties, it shall be lawful for the common council, board of aldermen, finance committee, or other governing body of such city or town, to pay such person so disabled as aforesaid, during the time he is disabled, such compensation, including medical attendance, as said common council, board of aldermen, finance committee, or other governing body of such city or town shall deem reasonable and proper, on the certificate of a physician, describing disabilities."

CHAPTER XVI.

AN EXCELLENT POLICE FORCE.

Summary of Events Compiled from Annual Reports—Distribution of the Force—Additional Men Appointed—A Mountain Tragedy.

PATERSON has always had an excellent police force. At present it consists of 88 men. The officers are a chief, captain, 7 sergeants, and 79 patrolmen. The oldest member of the police force is Chief Graul, who has served 26 years. Sergeant Keeff comes next with 25 years. Sergeant Hewitt and Patrolman Jordan each have 24 years and 6 months to their credit.

As in the case of the fire department, the writer has compiled the following summary of police history from the annual reports of the chief and the messages of the mayor. The official year ended March 20.

1876.—The mayor reported to the board of aldermen that the committee on police made some effort during the year to secure a better state of discipline and more effectiveness in the force than had heretofore existed. During the past year charges had been preferred against the chief for conduct unbecoming an officer. After a fair trial before the board of aldermen, it resulted in his removal from office, Feb. 14, 1876. Frederick G. Graul was appointed to fill the vacancy, April 3 following. The mayor recommended that the committee having charge of the department should give it their special attention, and whatever might be necessary to render the force efficient, well disciplined, and of high moral character, that the same be done.

1877.—The chief of police reported the discipline of the force as having been very good. But one officer had been reported with having violated the rules. The number of men on the force was twenty-five, consisting of the chief, four sergeants and twenty patrolmen. Attention was called to the unfit condition of the station house. Adjoining the room used for the police were the lodgers' rooms. In winter especially these rooms were always crowded at night with lodgers. Some plan, it was urged, should be adopted by which the policemen could be relieved from this unpleasant proximity to these lodgers.

The total number of arrests was 1,394.

The peace of the city had been very good, there having been no serious crimes or extensive robberies committed.

The distribution of the force was as follows: One sergeant to attend to licenses of saloons, pedlers, hacks, shows, &c. One patrolman to regulate the market for the sale of country produce. One patrolman for duty in the vicinity of the Erie Railway depot to prevent lounging about the depot and to protect passengers from being insulted in the waiting rooms, and to preserve the peace in that vicinity. Two patrolmen to do general patrol duty in the day time, and serve warrants, when issued, by the Recorder. One patrolman detailed at the station house in the day time to keep the police room and cells clean, attend all the wants of the station house, attend to the recorder's court while in session, and keep a correct list of persons apprehended, and their disposal by the recorder. One patrolman detailed at the station house in the night time to keep a correct list of persons applying at the station house for lodging, see that the lodging room was properly cleaned every morning, make a report of street lamps that had not been lighted during the night—when so reported by the officers going off duty every morning, make a report of all alarms of fire in the night time, the cause of the alarm, the box it is sent from and the exact time it strikes, and also deliver the fire lanterns to the officers doing duty at the fire. Three sergeants on night duty, each one having a district assigned him, to visit each patrolman as often as possible during the night, in their respective districts, make a written report every morning when going off duty, stating the time and place, when and where he saw each patrolman during the night, and report all irregularities on the part of any patrolman to the chief of police; also take charge of the police at fires where a fire occurs in their respective districts. Fourteen patrolmen to do night work, distributed as follows: One in the First ward, one in the Second ward, two in the Third ward, two in the Fourth ward, three in the Fifth ward, two in the Sixth ward, and three in the Seventh and Eighth wards. The city was divided into fourteen beats, whereby each patrolman had a very large territory to patrol.

1878.—The records of this year are missing.

1879.—There was a diversity of opinion in regard to the necessity of an increase of the force; it was a question that required to be carefully considered, the Mayor said. As a general rule the city was very peaceable, but it was thought advisable, if not necessary, to increase the force in order to shorten the beats.

On Monday, August 12, the body of Bartholomew McGrail was found beheaded, lying on the track of the N. Y., L. E. & W. R. R., near Passaic Bridge. It was rumored that he was murdered in this city and the body taken in a wagon to the spot where it was found. It was proved however that he came to his death by having been accidentally run over.

Four cases of highway robbery were reported during the year. A number of small burglaries were also committed.

The tramp had become a dangerous nuisance, and there were good reasons to believe that a great portion of the robberies committed in private dwellings were committed by them. The chief suggested that there be some plan adopted to put them to work, which would have the effect of driving them from the vicinity.

The force, he said, was entirely too small to guard the city against thieves and the young rowdy element that was growing up. It should consist of at least forty members.

The total number of arrests was 1,573.

1880.—Mayor Graham in his annual message indulged in some strictures on the misconduct of certain members of the force.

The principal object, he said, in maintaining a city was to protect the property and life of its citizens, and to do this there must be a well-organized and sufficient police force. He had suspended members of the force for various complaints. One member was dismissed. There were other complaints against some of the patrolmen, but the parties making the complaints were slow in coming forward to substantiate their charges. It had been shown during the year that a small number of the officers, by their misconduct, could weaken public confidence in the entire department. The city counsel had decided that the board of aldermen could make rules regulating the department. There was no branch of the city government, the mayor said, had met with such an amount of criticism as the police force. There had been a number of special policemen appointed, principally as private watchmen, whereby many points in the city had been guarded.

He recommended that the force be increased to at least its original number, as in his judgment it was too small for a proper surveillance of the largely increased floating population of the city.

On Saturday, June 28th, 1879, James Osborne was waylaid in a stable on Jersey street, and struck on the head with a cart rung in the hands of John Hartley, from which injuries he died three days afterward.

On the night of Oct. 28th, 1879, an old German named Michael J. Firchs, living in a shanty at No. 23 Ward street, was shot and killed.

On the evening of Monday, Sept. 15th, 1879, H. Corwin, of No. 51 Spring street, was assaulted near his residence, and robbed of his watch and chain.

On Saturday morning, Feb. 21st, 1880, the body of

Harriet Hink was found murdered in her apartments, No. 55 Division street. A jury brought in a verdict that she came to her death from injuries inflicted with a blunt instrument and they recommended that Patrick Henry Bracken be held for the action of the Grand Jury.

A great many burglaries had been committed during the year, principally in small stores and private houses.

On Sunday morning, May 2d, 1880, several German singing societies went to Garret Mountain at daybreak, as usual, to celebrate May-day. It drew together a great many people on the mountain, some of whom began strolling off on adjacent property. William Dalzell occupied a large plot of land next to the Garret Mountain property. A young man named Joseph Van Houten came on Dalzell's property. Dalzell's son and Van Houten began to quarrel, whereupon Dalzell, sr., shot the latter dead. The Dalzells fled to their dwelling, fearing violence. Officers hurried to the scene of the disturbance, and the murderer was arrested. The crowd set fire to the building, and the officers with their prisoner had to run across lots to the next house, to escape a shower of stones. Here several officers had very narrow escapes. The crowd showed a disposition to make an assault on the place. Two coaches were procured, one by the sheriff and one by the chief. The Rev. Father McNulty and the mayor went on the mountain and tried to pacify the enraged crowd. The priest volunteered to get on the seat with the driver. Dalzell was rushed from the house through the police lines to the carriage by the sheriff, and the carriage driven away, not, however, without the

FRANK VAN CLEVE.
POLICE JUDGE.

FREDERICK G. GRAUL.
CHIEF OF POLICE.

crowd making an unsuccessful attempt to capture the prisoner.

He was tried for manslaughter and a verdict of not guilty rendered.

As in the previous year, several robberies, of no great magnitude, were committed, the proceeds of which had been recovered.

The most extensive burglary committed for many years took place on the night of February 14th, 1881, in the jewelry establishment of Garside & Berdan, No. 122 Market street, and property carried away to the amount of $4,000.

Twenty-one additional men were appointed during the year, one resignation was received, and one officer was dismissed from the force during the year, making the total number of officers forty-three. The effect of more police officers was very apparent. There should be at least one officer to every thousand inhabitants. A great many more arrests had been made than in former years, and better order had been preserved, showing that the increase to the force had had the desired effect.

CHAPTER XVII.

CHANGES IN THE DEPARTMENT.

Homicides. Check Forgers, and Rioting—Thieves from Other Cities—Total Number of Arrests—Several Serious Shooting Affrays—A Terrible Explosion.

1882.—During the past year seven officers had been tried on charges. The mayor and citizens seemed to have worked themselves into a very uncomfortable state of virtuous indignation over the alleged delinquencies of a few black sheep in the department.

The mayor had a sermon to preach on this subject. He expressed himself as of the opinion that a change could be made for the better in the department, by promptly trying and disposing of all cases where charges were made against policemen. He had a plan, like all reformers. It was "that a change could be made for the better in trying all such cases, not in the method, but in the final ending of such trials, and to that end would recommend that hereafter the findings of the committee, upon the approval of the mayor, shall be ended."

If his plan, the mayor said, were adopted "it would have a tendency to increase the discipline of the force and relieve the aldermen from the pressure often brought to bear on them to shield an officer from a well deserved punishment."

The force consisted of chief, captain, four sergeants, thirty-eight patrolmen.

On April 25th, 1881, Patrolman John Bimson was promoted to be captain of police.

Value of stolen property restored, $2,235.85.

Total number of arrests, 3,083.

1883.—One homicide occurred during the year. It was committed on the night of August 15th, 1882, by David Taylor, who kept a liquor saloon at No. 85 Spruce street, his wife being the victim. He was convicted of manslaughter and sentenced to state prison for four years.

The city was visited the past year by three different sets of thieves from other cities: shoplifters and check forgers. Conviction followed arrest in every case.

The chief had ordered the force to be drilled twice a month in Upton's tactics, and thirteen department drills had been had, Captain Bimson being the instructor.

During the past year eleven men were appointed on the force, one resignation was tendered and one man was dismissed, making the total number 53.

Charges against members:

Patrolman Adam Hargreaves, neglect of duty; fine, 3 days.

Patrolman John W. McCrea, drunk; dismissed the force.

Patrolman Patrick Guilfoil; neglect of duty; one day's pay.

Patrolman John Sommers; disobedience of orders; reprimanded.

Patrolman Thomas Mullen; absent from duty; one day's pay.

1884.—The force numbered 48 men, as follows: 1 chief, 1 captain, 4 sergeants and 42 patrolmen.

The peace of the city had been very good during the preceding year. The timely arrival of Sergeant McBride with a squad of officers, on the evening of July 12th, on the corner of Main and Ellison streets, prevented what might have been a riot. The Orangemen's society had held a picnic at Bunker Hill. On their return in the evening an altercation took place between a hackman who was driving down Main street and a marshal of the Orangemen's procession. A large crowd gathered and but for the arrival of Sergeant McBride, a fight was inevitable.

A very serious accident occurred on July 13th, at the paint store of James F. Norwood and James D. Dunkerley, No. 474 Main street, which resulted in the loss of two lives. The accident was caused by the explosion of gas.

Three deadly assaults, one of them fatal, were recorded during the year.

The city covered over eight square miles of territory, and contained about 58,000 inhabitants. To cover this large territory and give proper police protection, it would require at least 75 men. It was deemed advisable to establish a sub station in the southern part of the city.

The aggregate amount of the pay roll was $44,594.11.

Total number of arrests, 3,136.

Total value of stolen property recovered, $1,752.88.

1885.—The force consisted of 1 chief, 1 captain, 4 sergeants and 40 patrolmen.

The captain took charge of the night force; each sergeant took charge of a squad of officers on post; three patrolmen were detailed for desk duty, two to serve warrants and answer calls for ambulance, and all other calls during the day time; one for duty at the depot in the day time; five for post duty in the forenoon in charge of a sergeant; ten for post duty in the afternoon, in charge of a sergeant, and nineteen for duty on post at night, in charge of two sergeants.

Officer Charles Hollaway died May 2d, 1884. He was appointed a patrolman, June 13th, 1870.

1886.—The mayor in his message declared that the force should be increased to at least one policeman to every thousand inhabitants.

Many burglaries had been committed, some of a serious character. In several cases business houses were entered, the safes blown open or the doors drilled, the combination locks destroyed, and in two cases (F. C. Van Dyek & Co.'s and H. B. Crosby & Son's) the burglars carried away a considerable amount of money and valuable papers.

Professional safe burglars worked very successfully about this time in all the cities of the Middle and Eastern States. Newark, Jersey City and Hoboken had been visited frequently by this class of thieves and all efforts to capture them had failed. Private houses and small store robberies had been quite prevalent during the fall and winter months, which caused extra duty to be imposed on the members of the force.

Several serious shooting affrays had occurred, one of which resulted in the killing of two persons, at the house No. 274 Main street; the husband killing his wife, and then killing himself. The parties to this tragedy were George Holford and Mary his wife. There were no witnesses, as the first intimation anyone had of its occurrence was when their son came home and found both dead. It was very plain to be seen from the surroundings that Holford had shot his wife in the head while she was asleep in bed, and then shot himself. He was a peddler by occupation and originally came from Newark, N. J.

On the night of August 15, 1885, John H. O'Dell went into the saloon kept by his wife at No. 25 1-2 West street and demanded an interview with her in the back room. She went in with him. He asked her if she would live with him again. She gave him a negative reply and came out into the bar room to serve customers. O'Dell came out behind her and stood at the end of the bar and without any warning pulled out a revolver from his pocket and fired two shots, one of which struck his wife in the breast, and the other grazed the head of one of the customers in the bar room. He was disarmed by one of the men present. O'Dell then ran to the police station and gave himself up to Officer Drew, who was on duty at the desk. O'Dell had served a term in the state prison for wife beating and had been discharged from that institution but a short time before the shooting. He was tried and convicted for attempting to commit murder and was sent to the state prison for five years. His wife soon recovered from her injury, the ball not having touched any vital part.

On October, 28th, 1885, another shooting affair occurred. This was at the law office of Z. M. Ward in the Vreeland building on Main street. This caused great excitement for a time on account of the parties to it being well known in the community. This was done by Thomas A. Dowling, who went to Ward's office, and while there shot Ward. Dowling fired two shots, one of which however only took effect. Dowling then ran to the police station and asked to be protected. It was at first supposed that Ward was fatally shot, but this proved not to be so, as he recovered very rapidly after the ball had been extracted from his person by his physicians.

1887.—The increase of thirty additional officers to the department during the past year had had a great influence over the young and lawless element, and had had the effect of breaking up a great deal of the corner lounging and other annoyances which were very prevalent.

The total number of arrests was 2,688.

1888.—A terrible explosion of a revolving rug boiler occurred at the Ivanhoe paper mill on April 23d, 1888, causing the death of two men and the injuring of about 20 other persons.

Among the list of casualties recorded in Chief Graul's report was a number of people who received injuries during the morning of March 12th, the day of the great blizzard.

The seven additional men appointed by the board

brought the number up to seventy-seven patrolmen, five sergeants, one captain, one chief.

The construction of the new lockup building during the past year was an improvement over the old structure, giving better lockup accommodation, better facilities for keeping clean and separating prisoners. This building, however, was only partly finished.

JOHN F. LEE,
CLERK.

JOHN BIMSON,
CAPTAIN.

CHAPTER XVIII.

PRESENT POLICE FORCE EXHIBIT.

The Most Horrible Murder Ever Committed in Paterson.—Many Petty Thefts.—Necessity of a Patrol Wagon.—Laws Concerning the Sale and Regulation of the Liquor Traffic.—Roster of the Department.

1889.—Two murders were committed, the victims being Matthew Ash, whose body was found in the river, near the West street bridge, on the afternoon of Nov. 8, and Kate or Cornelia Laber, who was murdered by her husband, Tunis, Feb. 28. This was, perhaps, the most horrible murder ever committed in this city, and was the result of jealousy.

The finishing and furnishing of the upper floor of the new headquarters' building the past year had given accomodations that the need of had been felt for a long time, and which were fully appreciated by the officers and patrolmen of the department. By this improvement the different grades of officers and patrolmen were separated from each other, each grade having their separate rooms. While there had been no extravagance shown in the furnishing of the different apartments, yet each was elegantly and substantially furnished.

1890.—Many petty thefts had been reported committed

by juvenile thieves. This class of thieving had increased wonderfully. Many of the arrests made and convictions had were of small boys. It was sometimes a hard problem for the judges of the county court to solve, when this class of offenders were brought before them, as to what disposition to make of them. Some were hardly fit subjects for the state reform school, yet some degree of restraint should be placed upon them. Many of this class fell into bad habits through neglect of their parents, who were compelled to work in the mills and workshops to earn their livelihood, while the children were left to themselves at home with no one to look after them. In this way they learnt to practice mischief, commenced pilfering, and soon cropped out as thieves. If a city or county institution were established where this class of offenders could be committed by the recorder for correction, many would, perhaps, have been saved from becoming habitual criminals.

The chief called attention to the fact that while the city had grown immensely in the past few years, both in population and improvement in property, the police force had diminished in numbers, and no effort had been made to increase the same. Whole blocks of dwelling houses and factories had grown up in the suburbs; the farm lands, where produce was raised a few years ago, had been transformed into homes of working people. The territory to be patrolled by the police had extended far out beyond where it was necessary to patrol before, yet the police force had not kept up with this growth, but had been reduced by death and dismissals; consequently, the police protection given the suburban parts of the city was limited, and of little effect. He therefore recommended that an additional number of men be appointed to meet this demand, and a sub-station be established in the southern part of the city; that provisions be made by which the ambulance and police vehicle be kept convenient to and under the direct supervision of the department, and that a police patrol wagon be purchased; all to be kept at the same place, with a man to take care of them. This, he said, would be a great improvement in the police and ambulance service, and the additional expense would be trifling.

1891.—Since the last annual report, the department sustained the loss of two men by death and one permanently disabled by sickness. No appointments had been made since July 18, 1887. At that time it was deemed necessary to appoint seven additional men, who made the total number of the force 77, consisting of chief, captain, 5 sergeants, and 70 patrolmen. Since that time two patrolmen were promoted to sergeants, five had died, one was dismissed from the force, and one was permanently disabled by sickness. This reduction brought the number of patrolmen down to 61 men. Of this number, three were detailed to desk duty in the station house, two to do detective work, serve warrants and answer calls; one as truant officer, one to do duty at railroad depot, and one to attend in the recorder's court. This reduction of the patrolling force reduced it to 53 men. The chief called attention to the necessity of providing the department with a patrol wagon. It was decided by the board last year to purchase one, but no provision was made as to where it should be kept, and the purchase was not made. The patrol wagon and ambulance, he said, should be kept in a stable connected directly with the police station, and a person should be engaged to take care of them both. He could see only one way by which that could be done, and that was to place them in the house occupied by Engine Company No. 1. That property could be directly connected with the station house by placing a door in the rear partition wall of that property. That house would be well adapted for that purpose. Then to provide a house for that company, a lot could be purchased next to their present house, and a house could be built for that company that would be better fitted for engine purposes than the house then used by them.

The department was also in great need of a fund on which to draw in cases that required the expenditure of money in following up criminals and violators of ordinances. He did not know of any police department that did not have such a fund. The department had never been provided with any funds to pay any expenses that were necessary to incur in either following up a criminal or obtaining evidence against violators of ordinances. The enforcing of the laws concerning the sale of liquor usually required some expense in obtaining evidence. The amount required was small, and when prosecutions were had and convictions followed, the amount so spent was usually returned ten-fold by fines imposed. Besides this, the state law required that all fees allowed by law in criminal cases for arrests, examinations, and serving commitments, shall be paid into the city treasury. This was done by the chief, monthly. The amount allowed by law for each arrest, under the criminal laws of the state, was 80 cents; for each examination, 50 cents, and for each commitment, $1. These bills were made payable to the city of Paterson, and were paid by the county collector. The amount collected annually from this source was usually from $800 to $1,000. The earning of this money was largely due to the persevering manner in which criminals were hunted down, and which oftentimes required some expense. It would therefore seem proper that some of the money derived from this source be set aside to meet such expenditures as were required to prosecute this work.

1892.—Following is an abstract of Chief Graul's annual report:

The peace of our city has been very good during the past year; we have had no severe disturbances of the peace, and no extensive robberies committed. The additional 15 patrolmen appointed by your honorable board in June last, and the two appointed to fill vacancies that occurred since that time, have made a good impression on the lawless element of this city, and was a wise step taken by you in the proper time. The patrol wagon which you have purchased, and goes into service now, will, I am sure, be one of the best appliances to do police work ever furnished this department. Yet the service of the patrol wagon will not be perfect until the police telegraph system is furnished. I therefore earnestly recommend that said system be furnished.

Two deaths have occurred in the membership of this

department during the past year, those of Patrolman William Beatty and Michael Phalon.

Patrolman Beatty was appointed a member of this department on June 17, 1872. He died Nov. 10, 1891, having thus served 19 years, 4 months, and 23 days.

Policeman Phalon was appointed on May 17, 1880. He died on Feb. 9, 1892, having thus served 11 years, 8 months, and 23 days.

ROSTER OF THE FORCE.—The following exhibit will show the name, age, date of appointment, and time served by each member of this department:

NAME.	AGE.	DATE OF APPOINTMENT.	TIME SERVED. Y'RS.	MO.
Frederick G. Graul	51	July 16, 1886	25	7
John Bimson	46	June 3, 1872	19	9
Henry Barclay	60	July 9, 1868	23	7
Michael Keeff	62	Oct. 21, 1867	24	4
James Hewitt	62	Nov. 18, 1867	24	3
John McBride	52	June 13, 1870	21	9
Adam Hargreaves	52	May 24, 1869	22	9
Mathew McGirr	37	July 10, 1882	9	8
John Riker	35	May 17, 1880	11	10
John Jordan	63	Nov. 18, 1867	24	3
John Rooney	65	May 24, 1869	22	9
Stephen H. Westervelt	58	June 13, 1870	21	8
Patrick Guilfoil	50	June 13, 1870	21	8
Wm. Wilds	53	May 6, 1872	19	10
John Cronk	62	June 3, 1872	19	9
Martin R. Drew	61	June 3, 1872	19	9
John Werger	54	June 3, 1872	19	9
Isaac Harris	54	May 17, 1880	11	10
Charles Magee	35	May 17, 1880	11	10

PRESENT POLICE FORCE EXHIBIT.

NAME.	AGE.	DATE OF APPOINTMENT.	TIME SERVED. Y'RS. MO.
John Powers	35	May 17, 1880	11 10
Wm. Roe	52	June 13, 1870	12 7
Frank Becker	50	May 17, 1880	11 10
James McNamara	48	"	11 10
Thomas McInerney	38	"	11 10
Thomas Mullen	36	"	11 10
John Sommers	37	June 21, 1880	11 9
David Kissick	41	July 10, 1882	9 8
Albert Magee	38	"	9 8
Jacob Struck	36	"	9 8
John Fields	47	"	9 8
Charles Schocklin	37	"	9 8
Benejah W. Beardsley	39	"	9 8
Wm. Bland	44	"	9 8
John Holland	32	"	9 8
Miles W. Fitzgerald	48	"	9 8
Peter Murphy	36	June 21, 1886	5 8
John W. Bradley	43	"	5 8
David Gibson	42	"	5 8
Thomas Walker	31	"	5 8
Patrick Kilt	43	"	5 8
Michael F. Bradley	31	"	5 8
Frank Bullock	35	"	5 8
Henry Vanderhoff	34	"	5 8
Patrick Fitzpatrick	42	"	5 8
John Rosenberg	38	"	5 8
Charles B. Bush	48	"	5 8
James Evers	30	"	5 8
Peter Zeluff	42	"	5 8
Andrew Vreeland	42	"	5 8
Andrew J. McBride	31	"	5 8
Charles F. Hopper	40	"	5 8

PRESENT POLICE FORCE EXHIBIT.

NAME.	AGE.	DATE OF APPOINTMENT.	TIME SERVED. Y'RS. MO.
Krine Overbeck	36	June 21, 1886	5 . 8
John McKelvey	32	"	5 . 8
Alexander Masterton	32	"	5 . 8
John Parkinson	34	"	5 . 8
George Halstead	33	"	5 . 8
John Romery	32	"	5 . 8
John Taylor	29	"	5 . 8
James Mullen	33	"	5 . 8
John Mullen	41	"	5 . 8
John Costello	40	"	5 . 8
Frank Whitta	43	"	5 . 8
Edward Nolen	34	July 18, 1887	4 . 7
Frank Zimmer	33	"	4 . 7
Howard Gall	33	"	4 . 7
Wm. H. Adams	44	"	4 . 7
Charles Titus	36	"	4 . 7
John D. Garrison	37	July 1, 1891	0 . 7
Wm. H. Lord	30	"	0 . 7
Henry O'Brien	23	"	0 . 7
George Cox	32	"	0 . 7
Adolph Keppler	28	"	0 . 7
Nelson Graham	38	"	0 . 7
John Draper	26	Sept. 1, 1891	0 . 5
Charles Robinson	28	"	0 . 5
John H. Hurd	38	"	0 . 5
James Miller	44	"	0 . 5
John Stewart	42	"	0 . 5
Wm. E. Perry	28	"	0 . 5
John Fielding	33	"	0 . 5
John Campbell	32	"	0 . 5
Daniel Dermond	34	"	0 . 5
Charles Boyle	32	Dec. 1, 1891	0 . 3

PRESENT POLICE FORCE EXHIBIT.

NAME.	AGE.	DATE OF APPOINTMENT.	TIME SERVED. Y'RS. MO.
Thomas J. McGrath	30	Dec. 27, 1881	0 2
James Dougherty	26	Mar. 1, 1892	0 0
Henry Titus	44	"	0 0
James Kehoe	26	"	0 0
Frank Sweetman	24	"	0 0

Total .... 88 men.

EXPENDITURES.

Amount of Pay Rolls.

For March, 1891	$ 5,626 24	For Sept., 1891	$ 6,697 29
" April "	5,483 35	" Oct. "	6,587 65
" May "	5,546 07	" Nov. "	6,474 01
" June "	2,538 90	" Dec. "	6,565 83
" July "	6,019 79	" Jan. 1892	6,595 53
" Aug. "	5,950 07	" Feb. "	6,571 50

Total pay rolls $73,656 32
Incidental expenditures 4,718 61

  Total expenditures $78,374 84

NUMBER OF ARRESTS MADE BY MONTHS.

For March, 1891	176	For Sept., 1891	261
" April "	180	" Oct. "	206
" May "	249	" Nov. "	189
" June "	259	" Dec. "	252
" July "	242	" Jan. 1892	191
" Aug. "	291	" Feb. "	180

2,676

CHAPTER XIX.

BIOGRAPHICAL SKETCHES.

Police Officials, Their Records and Services—The Executive Heads of the Department—They Are Men of Integrity and Experience, Who Have the Interest of the Public Welfare at Heart.

MAYOR Thomas Beveridge was born in Oneida county, New York, in 1840, where he received his early education. At the age of eighteen he left home and all his boyhood associates to try his fortune in the west. This was in 1858, and after knocking about the country for two years working on the farms of Michigan and other states, then mostly inhabited by Indians, he concluded there was no place like home and returned to New York state, where his folks were then living. When the war broke out in 1861 he enlisted in Company F, Twenty-sixth New York Volunteers. During the war he saw considerable active service, was wounded at the second battle of Bull Run, and was discharged shortly afterward, having won many laurels as a brave and valiant sergeant in the company in which he served. He was an able-bodied young man, noted among his companions for bravery and self-possession. At the close of the war he made his home in Brooklyn for a while, where he cast his first vote for President Lincoln, who was then running for a second term. The mayor, in speaking of the incident, says he will never forget standing in line for two hours while waiting his turn to cast a ballot for "Old Abe." This incident, coupled with the fact that it was on the 15th day of April, 1865, the day after Lincoln was assassinated, when Mr. Beveridge came to Paterson, fixes Lincoln and his eventful life indelibly in his memory.

His father, the late Thomas Beveridge, came to this city in 1863 and engaged extensively in the lumber business. The mayor joined his parents here a few years afterward and found employment with his father, whom he assisted for nine years. The elder Beveridge did a business of $250,000 a year. In the spring of '76 Thomas left his father, to embark in the coal business on his own responsibility. He located in Barclay street, where he has remained ever since, and now does a business of $50,000 yearly. As a business man he has made life a success. The strong Scotch nature, perseverance and endurance which he inherited from his father's side, has never deserted him in the most trying times. He is a man of remarkable vitality and constitutional vigor, and finds mental and manual labor alike easy. Being of a strong social nature, he seeks for companions among those who are generally considered foremost in business and political life. He is a self-made man in the full sense of the word, and so well balanced mentally that he can readily conform to any position, whether in business or politics. As a speaker he is slow and deliberate, a man of few words, never putting two where one will do, as his acceptance of the mayoralty nomination will show:

"Gentlemen of the convention, I feel highly honored by

your nomination, coming as it does, unsolicited. If elected I shall endeavor to perform the duties of the office to the best of my ability and the satisfaction of the people."

COMMISSIONER FRANK VAN CLEVE was born in the city of New York on January 24, 1853, and obtained his education in the public schools of the metropolis and the Free Academy, at present the Free College of the City of New York, graduated with honor at the latter institution. In 1869 he removed with his parents to Corona, a village near Hackensack, in Bergen county, N. J. Here he was ticket agent for the New York and New Jersey Railroad Company, and made himself useful on his father's farm. In June, 1875, he removed to Paterson where he entered the law office of Mr. John C. Paulison, he was admitted to the practice of the law in 1879, and Mr. Paulison dying shortly afterwards Mr. Van Cleve succeeded to his practice which he has since considerably increased. In April, 1886, he was appointed judge of the district court by Governor Green and served until January of the year following when a legislature differing from him in politics declined to re-appoint him. There are a number of sterling qualifications which have made Mr. Van Cleve one of the most popular men in the city. He is possessed of a genial good humor which is unruffled under the most adverse circumstances and this combined with his ready wit not only enlivens his conversation but also assists him materially in the exercise of his profession. He is gifted with legal acumen and a persuasive style of pleading which win him many cases and clients, and all who have ever had any dealings with him, know that he can be depended upon under all circumstances. He was appointed police justice by Governor Abbott in 1892, for a term of five years and is now holding the position.

COMMISSIONER JOHN MACDONALD was born at Philadelphia, Pa., April 16th, 1848; a resident of Paterson from 1854 until 1858 and from 1865 until the present time. When sixteen years old he enlisted for one hundred days in the 84th Regiment, N. G. S. N. Y., Colonel Conklin, After his discharge he re-enlisted for three years, or during the war, in 95th Regiment, N. Y. V. V. and was honorably discharged at the close of the war, having seen active service in front of Petersburgh, and taking part in the closing services that led up to the surrender of Lee's army, at Appomattox court house. In 1870 he joined Protective Engine Co., No. 5, of the Volunteer Fire Department of this city and was chosen secretary, assistant foreman and foreman of the company. In 1879 his company placed him in nomination before the Fire Department for the office of chief engineer, but he was defeated, the successful candidate at that time was B. Riley.

In 1883 his company, still true to him, once more made him their choice and the department ratified the choice by electing him without opposition. In 1888 he was elected alderman of the Third ward on the Republican ticket. In 1890 he was re-elected, the Democrats of the ward refusing to run a ticket against him. In 1890 at the organization of the board of aldermen he was elected president. In 1892, appointed police commissioner for one year; has been employed with Andrew, McLean & Co. during the past 25 years, and is now foreman in their weaving department at Passaic, N. J.

CHIEF OF POLICE FREDERICK G. GRAUL was born in Germany on Sept. 1st, 1840. His parents emigrated to this country when he was about nine years old, and settled in this city. He attended the public schools for several terms, and then was put to work in the mill. He worked at various occupations until the Civil war broke out when he enlisted on Sept. 17, 1861, in Company G, 7th Regiment, N. J. V., for three years. He participated in the siege of Yorktown, battle of Williamsburgh, Fair Oaks, Seven Pines, seven days' fight before Richmond, Bristo Station, second Bull Run, Fredericksburgh and Chancellorsville, Va. He was wounded at the last mentioned battle in the elbow of his right arm by a rifle ball. He participated in many small skirmishes which took place, and was taken prisoner in the seven days' fight before Richmond with four of his comrades. He was a prisoner for about six weeks, spending two weeks in tobacco warehouse No. three on Main street, Richmond, and the remaining four weeks on Belle Island, in the James River. At the end of that time he was exchanged and rejoined his regiment at Harrison's Landing, on James river. He was discharged Oct. 7th, 1864, at Trenton, N. J. He was appointed on the police force of this city July 16th, 1866, being one of ten men who were then appointed in organizing the first police force of this city. The ten men so appointed entered upon active duty Aug. 1st, 1866. He attended strictly to the business of that office, for which he was rewarded by promotion from time to time. His first promotion was given him by the city marshal, who was then chief of police, who made him temporary roundsman on Feb. 19th, 1867. He was made permanent roundsman on May 20th, 1867 by the board of aldermen. He was promoted to sergeant Sept. 12th, 1870; promoted to captain April 7th, 1873, and was nominated for chief of police by Mayor Benjamin Buckley, on April 3d, 1876, and received the unanimous vote of the board of aldermen for that appointment.

He has made many important arrests at various times. His first experience with criminals commenced on the night of Aug. 3d, 1866. It was the third night of active duty as a police officer. He had been detailed, with another officer named Henry Jones, to patrol that part of the city lying east from Carroll street, which was a suburban part of the city at that time, and which was known as the burglarized district on account of there having been numerous burglaries committed there previous to that time. Their instructions were to watch all the better class houses in that vicinity and endeavor to capture the thieves who were operating. They spent the greater part of their time near the corner of East Eighteenth street and Broadway. Jones had provided himself with a revolver, handcuffs and club; Graul had no revolver or handcuffs, but simply carried a small billet of wood. About midnight, on the third night of their watch, they discovered two men prowling around the house of A. B. Grant, situated on the south-east corner of East Eighteenth street and Broadway. Their actions indicated that they were burglars, intent on burlarizing that house. Graul and Jones tried to conceal themselves behind a rail fence on the opposite side of the street. The burglars, however, discovered the officers and endeavored to make their escape. One of them, the smaller man of the two, ran down Broadway toward the city, while the other, a very large and powerfully built man, remained standing in the middle of the road. Graul gave chase after the man down Broadway and after a short run captured him, placed him under arrest, and took him back to where Jones and the large man were standing. When he got within about one hundred feet of them, Jones left his man standing in the road and came and met Graul and his man. Jones took out his handcuffs and placed them on Graul's prisoner. Just then Jones' man started on a run out Broadway toward the country. Graul drew Jones' attention to it by saying: "Jones, there goes your man." Jones replied, "go and catch him." Sooner than let the man get away Graul again gave chase and ran the man down. The fellow, when he saw that Graul was close behind him, dropped on his hands and knees, thinking no doubt that the officer would fall over him. He was disappointed in this, however, as Graul had taken the precaution not to run right behind him, but a little to one side, and consequently when the man dropped Graul ran a few paces past him and turned to arrest him. The fellow was prepared for desperate work, and when he saw he had his match before him he opened fire from a large-sized Smith & Wesson revolver. Graul being unarmed had to resort to main force to subdue and capture the man. He therefore sprang at him and grappled to gain possession of the

MICHAEL KEEFF, Second Sergeant.
JOHN McBRIDE, Fourth Sergeant.   HENRY BARCLAY, First Sergeant.

burglars' weapon. During the struggle that ensued the weapon was discharged again. Graul then fought for the hand the burglar had the revolver in, and succeeded in getting hold of the weapon. The burglar fought with desperation, but when Graul had hold of the weapon he began using his stick on the burglar's head. The burglar cried "murder" and broke away and ran into the bushes, which were thick on both sides of the road. Graul ordered him to stop, and on his failing to do so the officer fired two shots at him, one of which took effect in the muscle of his right arm. Graul followed him into the bushes but could not find him. Jones, in the meantime, stood in the place where Graul left him, and made no effort to come and assist. He knew Graul had no revolver; he heard all that was going on; he heard the shots fired and knew it could not be his brother officer who was doing the firing, yet he was too cowardly to come near. This burglar made his escape that night but was arrested two days later at his house on Second avenue, in New York city, through information obtained from his partner. About thirty-six bills of indictment for burglary were found in this and Bergen county. They were tried and convicted on a number of those indictments, and were sentenced to twenty-seven years in state prison at Trenton. The names of this pair of thieves were Peter Reinhardt and Gustave Dorflinger. Reinhardt was a small-sized man and very cunning. Dorflinger was a very powerfully built man, and very desperate. He was a native of Switzerland and was about thirty-four years of age. His face, arms and body were covered with large scars. He escaped from the Trenton state prison in 1873, with five other convicts, and was recaptured a few days after the escape in Baltimore, Md., after having committed a burglary there. He was returned to Trenton prison and remained until the winter of 1885. He was then pardoned by the Court of Pardons, through the appeals made to the court by his relatives. He immediately went to Philadelphia and joined a gang of thieves known as the Fernwood gang. He was arrested, with other members of the gang, by Captain Quirk, Lieut. Beal, Detective Bond and Donoughy, of the Philadelphia Police Department, on March 15th, 1886, and gave them his name as Christopher Copaz. The gang was taken to Media, Delaware Co., Pa., where they had been operating. He was convicted of burglary and, on June 14th, 1886, received sentence of ten years in the Eastern penitentiary of Pennsylvania. Among those who escaped with Dorflinger from the Trenton prison in 1873 was one Charles Gray, alias Champagne Charlie, a five-year convict sent from this city. Chief Graul found him in Middletown, N. Y., and returned him to Trenton prison. Among the many arrests made by Chief Graul is one which he frequently refers to as being one in which he took desperate chances to prevent his prisoner from escapeing. This was a case where a notorious thief named Charles Conklin had robbed his employer of three hundred dollars and fled. The case was placed in Chief Graul's charge to look after, he being captain of police at that time. He could get no clue as to where Conklin had gone; he knew, however, that Conklin was well acquainted in some of the small North River towns. He consequently started out to make search for him in that direction. On Feb. 18th, 1875, his first place to make search was Haverstraw, N. Y. He immediately upon his arrival there learned that Conklin was stopping at an hotel there, but had gone out sleigh riding with a friend and two girls, but he could not ascertain what direction they had gone in. He obtained the services of a constable of Haverstraw, and he recommended that they hire a team and go hunting the country hotels for them. This plan was adopted and the man who furnished and drove the team guaranteed that he would find Conklin or he would make no charge. They drove many miles and visited many country hotels until at midnight they drove under the shed of Knapp's hotel at Clarksville and there found the team that Conklin had hired. Graul went into the bar room of the hotel and arrested him. Conklin laughed and said, "I am in New York State and you have no business here." Graul replied, he would not be in that state long, and proceeded to take Conklin outside and place him in the sleigh. Conklin asked to be allowed to get his things which were in the upper part of the house. He went up with Conklin and the women of the house and the crowd in the bar room followed. As soon as Conklin got into the room, he refused to go and began to show fight. The proprietors of the hotel urged the crowd not to allow Conklin to be taken, and some move was made by the crowd to force themselves into the room. Graul, seeing that he had to resort to desperate means, pulled his revolver and cleared the room, and handcuffed Conklin. He placed him in the sleigh and took him to the house of the constable at Haverstraw, and waited to take the first train in the morning. Conklin first refused to come out of New York state without a requisition, but finally consented to come provided Graul did not handcuff him. This was agreed to, and Graul left Haverstraw with his prisoner on the first train on the New York and New Jersey railroad. When they had gone for some distance, Conklin became sick and wanted to go to the closet. Chief Graul went with him and remained at the door with it partly open. Conklin was inside watching his chance to close the door entirely. He succeeded in doing this eventually, the catch being on the inside. Graul could not open it. Conklin opened the window and dropped on the frozen snow. He rolled over several times and came near getting under the wheels. Graul stepped out on the platform of the cars just in time to see Conklin pick himself up and start off on a run. The train was running at the rate of about twenty miles an hour according to Conductor Ball's judgment. When the officer saw Conklin pick himself up and run, he swung his body off from both hand rails and jumped, and slid on the snow for some distance. He threw off his heavy overcoat and went in pursuit of Conklin over the frozen snow. He caught him again after a chase of about five hundred yards. The train had gone on and Graul had to walk his prisoner to the next station, which was Hillsdale. He arrived home with his prisoner all right, and in due time sent him to Trenton for three years.

Chief Graul has always showed great activity as a police officer. He has brought fugitives from many places outside of this state, namely, Pittsburg, Philadelphia, Reading and Allentown, Pa., Holyoke and Springfield, Mass., Port Jervis, Middletown, Goshen, Brooklyn, Yonkers and New York city. He entered the service at the age of twenty-six and is now in his fifty-third year.

THOMAS C. SIMONTON, JR. was born in the city of New York, but before he was a year old his parents removed to Paterson, and he has resided here ever since. In 1874 he entered the office of Hon. G. A. Hobart as a law student, and in June of 1877, he was admitted to the bar of New Jersey as an attorney; in June, 1880, after the expiration of the necessary three years of additional study, he was admitted as a counsellor at law of the state. Mr. Simonton is also an attorney and counsellor at law of the state of New York, and at times practices law there. In 1887 he was appointed city counsel of Paterson for one year, and in 1888 was re-appointed to the same office for a period of five years. He is an active member of the Republican party. Mr. Simonton has a fine law practice and that combined with his office as city counsel, makes him an extremely busy man.

STATE SENATOR JOHN HINCHLIFFE has effected much for the Police and Fire departments in the way of important and needful legislative enactments, looking towards the improvement of these organizations. He is the steady friend of these and all other public interests in Paterson, which come under his official cognizance.

Senator Hinchliffe was born in New York city, May 19th, 1850, and has resided in Paterson since he was one year old. He is president of the Hinchliffe Brewing and Malting company of Paterson. He was educated in the public schools. He was a member of the board of education of Paterson from 1875 to 1877, and a commissioner of taxes and assessments for two terms, from 1877 to 1881, and was president of the board during his last term.

James C. Sigler was born Sept. 1st, 1848, in the city of New York, but became a resident of Paterson three months later where he has always resided at the one place, 21 Washington street, in the Third ward. He has always been identified with the political fortunes of the Democratic party. He was a member of the first county board of registration and was reappointed for the second term. He is at present business manager of the Paterson *Daily Guardian*, the oldest paper in Passaic county and the only Democratic daily paper in the city. He has been employed on this paper, on and off, for 33 years, filling every position from newsboy to his present responsible position. He was appointed a member of the police commission at the formation of the board in March, 1892.

Police Commissioner William Ryan was born in Paterson, N. J., fifty years ago. When a boy he received an ordinary school education and afterward learned the trade of carriage painter. He worked in the locomotive works for a time, painting the cabs and tenders of locomotives. He afterward engaged in the carriage-painting business for himself and established a large, remunerative business by

CHAPTER XX.

GENERAL RULES, POLICE DEPARTMENT.

How the Force is Governed and Disciplined—Their Duties Defined—
A Formidable Machine That is Controlled with the Simplicity and
Regularity of Clock-work.

ONE. Each and every member of the police force shall devote his whole time and attention to the duties of his office, and is expressly prohibited from following any other calling, or being employed in any other business. Although certain hours may be allotted to the respective members for the performance of duty on ordinary occasions, yet at all times they must be prepared to act immediately on notice that their services are required.

2. Punctual attendance, prompt obedience to orders, and conformity to the rules of the department, will be rigidly enforced.

3. Each and every member in his conduct and deportment must be quiet, civil and orderly; in the performance of his duty, he must maintain decorum and attention, command of temper, patience and discretion; he must at all times refrain from harsh, violent, coarse, profane, or insolent language, yet at the same time, when required, act with firmness and sufficient energy to perform his duty.

4. No member of the department shall, in the station-house or elsewhere while on duty, drink any kind of liquor,

or *smoke*, or (except in the immediate performance of his duty) *enter any place in which any kind of intoxicating drink may be sold or furnished*. No liquor, or any intoxicating drink, shall, upon any pretext, be introduced into the station-house, except as advised by a physician; nor shall smoking by any member of the force be allowed at any time in the station-house.

5. No member of the police force shall receive or share in, for his own benefit, any present, fee, gift or emolument for police service other than the regular salary, except by consent of the police committee; nor shall any such member receive or share in any fee, gift or reward from any person who may become bail for the appearance of any arrested, accused or convicted person, or who may become surety for any such person on appeal from the judgment or decision of any court or magistrate, or any fee, gift or reward in any case, from any attorney-at-law who may prosecute or defend any person arrested or prosecuted for any offense within the county of Passaic; but policemen may receive to their own use their ordinary fees as witnesses, when entitled thereto, on subpœnas, except in the recorder's court.

6. No member of the department will be permitted to apply for a warrant in any court, or make a complaint for damages, or adjust the same, unless he shall have received permission from the chief of police.

7. No member shall compound any offence against the law, or withdraw any complaint.

ADAM HARGREAVES, 5th Sergeant.   JOHN RIKER, 7th Sergeant.
JAS. HEWITT, 3d Sergeant.   MATHEW McGIRR, 6th Sergeant.

GENERAL RULES.

8. No member shall communicate to any person any information which may enable persons to escape from arrest or punishment, or to dispose of or secrete any goods or other valuable things stolen or embezzled.

9. No member shall communicate, except to such persons as directed by his superior in office, any information respecting orders he may have received, or any regulation that may be made for the government of the department.

10. Each member shall at all times have with him a small book in which he shall enter the names of persons taken in charge by him, and such particulars in each case as may be important in the trial thereof.

11. The chief of police and captain, sergeants and patrolmen when on duty shall wear the shield on the outside of the outermost garment, over the left breast.

12. Policemen shall at all times, and on all occasions when on duty, conspicuously display their shields so that the entire surface of the same may be easily and distinctly seen.

13. Any persons who shall be arrested shall be taken immediately before the recorder, or to the station-house; and the officer making the arrest shall report to the officer in charge the name of the party arrested, and the cause and time of the arrest.

14. The night policemen, when off duty, in case of fire shall immediately repair to such fire, and report to the chief of police, or in his absence, to the senior officer present; and on occasions of fires, riots, or emergencies when the reserve force has been on active duty, the officer in

charge, immediately on their return to the station-house, shall call the roll, to ascertain who, if any, have been absent.

15. Members of the police force must be civil and respectful to each other on all occasions. Courtesy in the intercourse between officers and members of the force promotes discipline, and tends to produce mutual respect. A patrolman on meeting or passing a superior officer shall salute him in the manner prescribed for "Officer's Salute" in Upton's Military Tactics. It is the duty of the subordinate to offer *first* the prescribed salutation, and of the superior to return it. Men in the ranks will not salute unless ordered to do so by the officer in command. Members of the force on duty in citizen's dress are not required to salute.

16. They must not render any assistance in civil cases, except to prevent an immediate breach of the peace, or to quell disturbance actually commenced.

17. Every member of the force will be furnished with a copy of the rules and regulations, which they will keep in their possession, in order to become perfectly familiar with their respective duties.

18. All members of the force who find horses or cattle astray, must report the same to the officer in charge at the station-house, who will cause the same to be taken to the public pound.

19. Members of the department when suspended, or on resigning, will immediately surrender their book of rules and regulations, their shield, wreath and other insignia of office in their possession, to the chief of police.

which he accumulated considerable property. He always took an active part in politics, being a staunch Democrat and a liberal contributor. He was elected five times for two-year terms to represent the Seventh ward in the board of aldermen. He was appointed a police commissioner in March, 1892, and was chosen the first president of the board of police commissioners. He has been an energetic worker in all positions of public trust, and always enjoyed the confidence of his constituents.

JOHN F. LEE was born at Carbondale in the state of Pennsylvania, in the year 1859. He came to Paterson with his parents when two years of age, and has resided here ever since. After receiving the usual public school education he entered the employ of Hamil & Booth and remained in their employ until he was twenty years of age. After leaving the silk business Mr. Lee entered the employ of the Prudential Life Insurance Co. He acted as agent for the company for about seven years, when he was promoted to the position of assistant superintendent. He retained this position for two years, when he left the employ of the Prudential Co. to engage in the business of real estate and insurance agent, in which business he has been engaged continuously ever since. Mr. Lee has been successful in the real estate and insurance business. He has always been a staunch Democrat, and in the year 1889 he was elected on the Democratic ticket as a justice of the peace to represent the seventh ward. Mr. Lee has always been identified with the C. Y. M. L. A. the most successful Catholic association in the city of Paterson, and for the past two years has been its president. Mr. Lee was appointed clerk of the police court and also clerk of the board of police commissioners in March, 1892.

20. No member of the department shall leave the city or be absent from duty, without permission from the chief of police.

21. Unless in cases of sickness contracted while on the police force and so certified by the city physician, absence from duty of any member thereof, without due leave, shall be considered cause for removal or forfeiture of pay for the time absent, as the board of aldermen in the first case, or the committee on police in the second case, may determine.

22. In case of the sickness of any member of the police force, and his inability thereby to be on duty, he shall at the earliest possible moment notify the chief of police thereof, procure a certificate from a reputable physician of the city of Paterson, or deliver to the chief of police a sworn statement of his illness.

23. Every member when entering on duty must be neat in his person, with his clothes and boots clean, and his dress in conformity with the regulations.

24. No policeman shall connect himself with any society, club, committee, or organization of any kind, the object of which is the political advancement of any political party, clique or individual, or be a member of any fire or military corps.

25. No member of the department will be allowed to receive any complimentary subscription or gift, whether tendered by citizens or any member of the police force.

26. No member of the department shall be permitted to solicit or make any contributions in money or other thing,

on any pretext, to any person, committee or association, for any political purpose whatever.

27. CHIEF OF POLICE.—The chief of police shall keep an account of all property, money or valuables stolen and that may come to his possession, in whose possession the same is found, and when reclaimed shall take a receipt under said account of all such property reclaimed, and if the same is not reclaimed in three months, shall turn the same over to the mayor, to be by him disposed of as the board of aldermen may direct.

28. The chief of police shall, at the first regular meeting in every month, report to the board of aldermen the number of arrests made during the month previous thereto, by whom such arrests were made, the nature of the offence, and any other matter pertaining to his office, which he may deem proper to report upon. He shall also render a full report, in writing, of the duties of his office for the preceding year, at each annual meeting of the board of aldermen.

29. The chief of police shall keep a book, wherein shall be entered the name and residence of each policeman; also a roll showing the time of night each policeman shall go on duty, the beat on which he is stationed, and his hours of actual duty; and shall note the absentees at each roll-call.

30. The chief of police shall keep in his office a book in which shall be entered the name of every person complained of for violation of the city ordinances, the nature of the complaint, and the name and residence of the complainant in each case, and shall make a report thereof to the

committee on police as often as they shall require, and to the board of aldermen once a month.

31. The chief of police shall designate the day and night posts in each ward, and the policemen who are to patrol the same.

32. It shall be the duty of the chief to repair in person to all serious or extensive fires, to all riots or tumultuous assemblages within the city, and take command of the police present; to save and protect property, and to arrest such persons as he may find disturbing the peace, or inciting so to do.

33. It shall be his duty to communicate to the city physician the presence of any contagious or infectious disease, or the existence of any nuisance in the city, which shall be detrimental to public health.

34. It shall be the duty of the chief to see that the laws of the state and the ordinances of the city are duly enforced throughout the city, and it shall also be his duty to instruct each member of the police force as to his duty under the rules of the police department, the ordinances of the city and the laws of the state; and to see that each member becomes familiar with said rules and ordinances, and to report any delinquency in that respect to the mayor or the committee on police.

35. He shall keep a book in which shall be recorded all orders promulgated by him; he shall post a copy of each general order issued by himself on a bulletin in the assembly room; and he shall cause copies of the same to be fur-

nished to the committee on police from time to time as often as they shall require.

36. He shall promptly report to the mayor each and every case of dereliction of duty of any member of the department, which may in any way come to his knowledge, and also all complaints made to him against any member thereof.

37. All members of the police force shall be considered to be always on duty, and shall appear in full uniform, except when the mayor or committee on police shall deem it proper to allow them to appear in citizen's dress.

38. CAPTAIN OF POLICE.—During the illness or absence of the chief of police, the captain of police shall execute and discharge the duties of the office of chief of police, and at all other times shall perform such duties as may be prescribed.

39. He shall promptly report in writing to the chief of police every case of dereliction of duty of any member of the department, which report shall contain the name of the person reported, and the nature of the offense or charge against him.

40. SERGEANTS.—Each and every sergeant shall, if possible, see each patrolman on his beat within his district, without calling; but should he not be able to find one, the call will be given in the center and on each extremity of the beat, and if unable then to find the man he is in search of, he will extend his search to the adjoining beats, until the beat of the man absent is fully re-covered. He will report

to the chief of police the name of the man and the cause of absence, if ascertained.

41. The sergeants must report to the officer in charge at the station house every morning, before seven o'clock, the time and place where they saw and conversed with the patrolmen in their respective districts during the several hours of patrol duty performed by them, and in what manner they were occupied when so visited.

42. The sergeants' reports on the location of patrolmen shall cover intervals of not more than two hours' time, unless for satisfactory reasons; and the sergeants shall make oath before the recorder, on the first day of each month, to the correctness of their reports made daily during the preceding month.

43. The sergeants shall carefully note every case of misconduct or neglect of duty of the patrolmen belonging to their respective districts, and report the same to the chief of police.

44. PATROLMEN.—The prevention of crime being the most important object in view, the patrolmen's exertions must be constantly made to accomplish that end. They must examine, and make themselves perfectly acquainted with, every part of their respective beats, and vigilantly watch every description of persons passing their respective ways. They must, to the utmost of their power, prevent the commission of assaults, breaches of the peace, and all other crimes about to be committed.

45. They must, by their vigilance, render it extremely difficult for anyone to commit crime in their respective

beats. The absence of crime will be considered the best proof of the efficiency of the police, and when on any beat offences frequently occur, there will be good reason to suppose that there is negligence or want of ability on the part of the person in charge of such beat.

46. They shall carefully inspect every part of their respective beats, but the regularity of inspection hereby enjoined shall not prevent any of them from remaining at any particular place, if their presence be required; and if they so remain, they must satisfy their superior officer that there was sufficient cause for their so doing.

47. They must at all times be able to furnish particular information respecting the state of their respective beats.

48. They shall frequently, during the tour of patrol duty, carefully examine, in the night time, all doors and low windows of dwelling houses and stores in their respective beats, to see that they are properly secured; also areas and area gates of the several houses within such beats.

49. They must, if possible, fix in their minds such impressions as will enable them to recognize suspicious persons whom they frequently meet in the streets at night, and endeavor to ascertain their names and residences, and communicate to their commanding officer all information concerning them.

50. They shall strictly watch the conduct of all persons of known bad character, and do so in such manner that it will be evident to such parties that they are watched and that certain detection must follow the attempt to commit crime. They shall note the time in writing of the appear-

JOHN HINCHLIFFE,
SENATOR.

ance of any person of known bad character on their respective beats, the attending circumstances, and the premises that such persons may enter, and report to the commanding officer.

51. They shall report to the chief of police all gamblers, receivers of stolen property, or their suspicions that certain persons are such.

52. When any person charges another with the commission of a crime, and insists that the person charged shall be taken into custody, the policeman shall require the accuser, if unknown to him, to accompany him as a witness, along with the accused, to the police station, and shall then with as little delay as possible return to his beat and inspect the same with great care, to see that no depredations have been committed during his absence.

53. They shall carefully watch all disorderly houses, or houses of ill fame, or houses which disorderly persons frequent, within their respective beats, observe by whom they are frequented and report their observations to their commanding officer.

54. They shall pay particular attention to all ale houses, hotels, saloons or restaurants, which close at unusually late hours, and are kept open between twelve o'clock on Saturday night and twelve o'clock on Sunday night, and report the same to the chief of police.

55. They shall take particular notice of all hacks, cabs or other vehicles at night which under any circumstances excite their suspicions.

56. Neither of them shall leave his beat until regularly relieved, unless it be for the purpose of taking a prisoner to the station house, or to answer a call for assistance by a police officer, or to make an arrest in view on the confines of his beat, or to follow an offender to an adjoining beat for the purpose of making an arrest.

57. They shall examine carefully all street lamps on their respective beats, and report to their commanding officer all that may not be lighted at the proper time, are not properly cleaned, or are in any way out of order.

58. If any of them shall observe in the street anything likely to produce danger or public inconvenience, or anything which seems irregular or offensive, they shall report the same immediately on their return to the station house.

59. Each and every one of them shall give his name and number to all persons who may require the same.

60. They must not use the baton except in the most urgent cases of self-defense.

61. Policemen must not walk together, or talk with each other, or with any other person when they meet on the confines or any other part of their beats, unless it be to communicate information appertaining to the department, and such communication shall be as brief as possible.

62. They must constantly patrol their respective beats while on duty, unless otherwise directed by the rules and regulations of their commanding officer.

63. It will be deemed a neglect of duty on the part of a policeman carelessly to lose his shield, emblem, or other insignia of office, or neglect to fasten the same securely to

his person, or when lost not to report the same immediately thereafter to the officer in command at the station house.

64. Umbrellas or walking canes are not to be used by policemen while on duty.

65. Each policeman holds his office during good behavior only. It is therefore especially enjoined upon members of the department carefully to study and thoroughly understand the police rules, and to acquire a sufficient knowledge of the laws and ordinances of the city to enable them to discharge their respective duties.

66. UNIFORMS.—The full dress of the members of the police force shall be of navy blue cloth, indigo dyed and all wool, of the standard make and quality used by the New York city police force.

67. The style of the dress shall be as follows: For the officers:—A double-breasted frock coat; waist to extend to the top of the hips; skirt within one inch of the bend of the knee; two rows of buttons on the breast, eight in each row, placed equal distances from each other; distance between each row, five and a half inches at the top, three and a half inches at the bottom; rolling collar; cuffs three and a half inches deep, three small buttons on the under seam; two buttons on the hips, one button on the bottom of each skirt pocket welt, two buttons intermediate, so that there shall be six buttons on the back; lining of the coat black; pantaloons plain; vest single-breasted, with nine buttons placed at equal distances from each other.

68. For the patrolmen:—Single-breasted frock coat; rolling collar; waist to extend to the top of the hip, skirt to

within one inch of the bend of the knee; nine buttons on the breast; two buttons on the hips; two buttons on the bottom of each pocket, and three small buttons on the under seam of the cuffs; pantaloons to have white welt on the outer seam; vest single-breasted, with nine buttons placed at equal distances from each other.

69. The summer dress shall consist of navy blue flannel sack coat, and navy blue flannel pantaloons, indigo dyed and all wool, of the standard make and quality known as the Middlesex flannel. The style for the officers shall be double-breasted coat, buttoned close up to the chin; short rolling collar; two rows of buttons of five each on the front; coat to reach half way between the hip and knee; pantaloons to be without welt in the seam. The style of this dress for the patrolmen shall be single-breasted sack, buttoned close up to the chin, to reach half way between the hip and knee; four buttons on the front; no pockets to show on the outside; pantaloons to be same as in winter.

70. The overcoat shall be of blue cloth, indigo-dyed, double-breasted, rolling collar, waist to extend to one inch below the hip, skirt to three inches below the bend of the knees; swell edge, stitched one-fourth of an inch from the edge. The chief of police and the captain will have nine police buttons on each breast, six on back and skirt, and three on the cuffs. Patrolmen will have nine police buttons on each breast, four on the back and skirt, and two on the cuffs. All buttons on the breast of double-breasted coats shall be placed in two rows, at a distance between rows of seven inches at top and three and a half inches at

bottom, measured from centers, and in such manner as to form, when the coat is buttoned, direct lines from top to bottom. The material of the overcoat shall be of the standard quality and make used by the New York city police force.

71. The hats, caps, badges, buttons, batons, clubs, etc., shall be such as the committee on police may adopt, samples of which shall be deposited in the office of the chief of police.

72. All officers when on active duty shall wear standing collars of sufficient depth to show one-fourth of an inch above the coat collar, and black neck dressings. The day patrol shall wear white gloves while on their posts. Coats shall be worn buttoned at all times during active out door duty, and the club or baton shall be habitually carried in the hand.

73. STATION HOUSE REGULATIONS. No person shall be allowed to remain in the station house without express permission from the officer in charge, except members of the department and persons on business.

74. The officer in command at the police station house shall enter in a book to be there kept for the purpose, the name at full length of every person detained therein, the time of his arrest, the offence with which he may be charged, the name and residence of the complainant, and the name of the officer or patrolman that arrested said person.

75. He shall also enter in a book to be kept at the said station house an account of all property, money or other

valuable thing which may come into his possession, the name and residence of the owner, if known, in whose possession it was found, and by whom, and whether the same was stolen or otherwise.

76. He shall transmit copies of the entries made pursuant to the two preceding rules to the chief of police every morning at 9 o'clock, together with the time and cause of taking said person into custody, and the names and residences of the witnesses.

77. There shall be kept at the station house, for the use of the criminal authorities, under the direction of the chief of police:

1st. A record of orders issued from his office.

2d. A record of suspicious persons and places in the city of Paterson.

3d. A record of reported crimes and misdemeanors committed in the city of Paterson, for which no arrests have been made at the time they are reported.

4th. A record of houses of prostitution, assignation houses, gambling houses, and disorderly or disreputable houses of every kind in the city of Paterson, with the names of the owners and keepers thereof.

78. The members of the force shall assemble at the station house for drill, according to Upton's Manual of Military Tactics, in the "School of the Soldier" without arms, whenever so ordered by the chief of police or as often as in his judgment necessity requires.

CONTENTS.

CONTENTS.

CHAPTER I.

"THE LYONS OF AMERICA."

What a Century Has Done for Paterson—Alexander Hamilton—The "Society for Establishing Useful Manufactures."—The First Cotton Mill—Business Development of the City—The Great Falls. . . . . PAGE 5

CHAPTER II.

SKETCH OF THE OLD FIRE DEPARTMENT.

An Organization That Did Notable Service and Produced a Devoted Body of Men—Their Services Briefly Reviewed—Introduction of the Steam Engine—Some Big Fires. 12

CHAPTER III.

CHIEFS AND ASSISTANT ENGINEERS.

Past and Present Department Commanders—A Roster of Well-known Names—Date of Appointment and Term of Service. 23

CHAPTER IV.

ENGINE AND HOSE COMPANY SKETCHES.

When Organized and Where Located—The Goose-neck and Piano-box Engines—The Amoskeag—The Silsby—Modern Apparatus—Hose and Hook and Ladder Companies 28

CONTENTS.

CHAPTER V.

A CITY ORDINANCE, 1875.

Providing for the Regulation, Management and Government of the Department—Elections, How Conducted—Officers and Elections—Duties and Responsibilities.................. 36

CHAPTER VI.

DIGEST OF SOME ANNUAL REPORTS.

Views of the Mayor and Chief Engineer—Looking toward a Paid Fire Department—Recommending the Purchase of a Steam Fire Engine—The Last Hand Engine.................. 39

CHAPTER VII.

DISAPPEARANCE OF THE HAND ENGINE.

Employment of Horses for Moving of Engines—Improved Steam Apparatus—Membership of the Department—Fire and Alarms—Chief Stagg Complimented.................. 44

CHAPTER VIII.

A PAID FIRE DEPARTMENT.

The Volunteers Are Succeeded by the Present System — Radical Changes — Increased Expenditures — Efficiency of the Service Increased—Modern Methods and Scientific Appliances..... 50

CHAPTER IX.

PRESENT STATUS OF THE DEPARTMENT.

Officers—Apparatus—Engine, Truck and Hose Companies—The Men and Their Work—How the Companies Are Manned and Officered—Valiant Fire Fighters.................. 59

CHAPTER X.

THE BENEVOLENT ASSOCIATION.

Its Organization and Reorganization — Past and Present Officers—Its Beneficiary Features — Widows and Orphans — Rules and Regulations.................................... 65

CHAPTER XI.

THE EXEMPT ASSOCIATION.

The Plan of Organization—Permanent Officers—Fair at Washington Hall—Installed in Its New House—Present Affairs of the Association—A Burial Clause Inserted in the By-Laws......... 68

CHAPTER XII.

BIOGRAPHICAL SKETCHES.

Some of the Officers of the Old and New Departments Who Have Made Fire History—Chief Stagg and His Staff—Exempt Veteran Firemen Whose Names Are Household Words.......... 72

CHAPTER XIII.

RULES AND REGULATIONS OF THE FIRE DEPARTMENT.

Fire Department Officials—Qualifications of Members—Pay of the Force—Badges and Uniforms—Insignia of Office—Fire Alarm Telegraph—Burial Fund Association.............. 83

CHAPTER XIV.

ORGANIZATION OF THE POLICE FORCE.

A Record of Police Protection Written by Chief Graul—Some Exciting and Interesting Episodes Officially Related—The Force Up to Date.................................... 101

CONTENTS.

CHAPTER XV.

THE AMENDED CHARTER.

An Oath of Affirmation—The Mayor to Appoint All Policemen, Subject to the Confirmation of the Board of Aldermen—A Chief of Police—A Day and Night Police Force—Their Duties and Compensation—Chief, Captain, Sergeants and Patrolmen—Uniform and Badges—Salary 111

CHAPTER XVI.

AN EXCELLENT POLICE FORCE.

Summary of Events Compiled from Annual Reports—Distribution of the Force—Additional Men Appointed—A Mountain Tragedy. .115

CHAPTER XVII.

CHANGES IN THE DEPARTMENT.

Homicides, Check Forgers, and Rioting—Thieves from Other Cities—Total Number of Arrests—Several Serious Shooting Affrays—A Terrible Explosion 122

CHAPTER XVIII.

PRESENT POLICE FORCE EXHIBIT.

The Most Horrible Murder Ever Committed in Paterson.—Many Petty Thefts.—Necessity of a Patrol Wagon.—Laws Concerning the Sale and Regulation of the Liquor Traffic.—Roster of the Department 129

CHAPTER XIX.

BIOGRAPHICAL SKETCHES.

Police Officials, Their Records and Services—The Executive Heads of the Department—They Are Men of Integrity and Experience, Who Have the Interest of the Public Welfare at Heart 138

CHAPTER XX.

GENERAL RULES, POLICE DEPARTMENT.

How the Force is Governed and Disciplined—Their Duties Defined—
A Formidable Machine That is Controlled with the Simplicity and
Regularity of Clock-work.................. 151

ADVERTISEMENTS.

BAMFORD BROS.'

Silk Manufacturing Company.

"CRESCENT MILLS," Cliff St.
"ALBION MILLS," Madison St.

THE LARGEST ALL-SILK RIBBON
MANUFACTURERS IN
THE WORLD.

Paterson, N. J.

LOUIS F. LIOTARD,

SUCCESSOR TO A. LIOTARD,

Manufacturer and Importer of all kinds of

REEDS AND HARNESS.

SOLE AGENT FOR CHAISE FRERES' PATENT BRAIDED HEDDLES.

50 and 52 Essex St., Paterson, N. J.

Telephone No. 387.

Pelgram & Meyer,

MANUFACTURERS OF

SILKS, RIBBONS, ETC.

Factories at Paterson, N. J., Boonton, N. J., and Harrisburg, Pa.

SALESROOM, 58 & 60 GREENE ST., NEW YORK.

P. O. Box 808.

J. ATKINSON & CO.,

MANUFACTURERS OF

BOBBINS, SPOOLS, ETC., of Every Description Used in Manufacturing.

Job Turning done of All Kinds.

95, 97 and 99 RIVER STREET, - - PATERSON, N. J.

(Near Main Street Bridge.)

WM. H. DUNKERLY,

MANUFACTURER OF

Cotton, Woolen, Flax and Silk Machinery,

FLUTING ROLLERS OF EVERY DESCRIPTION.

SPECIAL: PATENT REELS AND PATENT DOUBLERS.

Dealers in New and Second-Hand Machinery; Engines, Boilers, Steam Pumps, Injectors, Shafting, Pulleys, Hangers, etc.

COR. SPRUCE AND GRAND STS.,   PATERSON, N. J.

Doherty & Wadsworth,

MANUFACTURERS OF

Handkerchiefs,

Ribbons,

Grenadines, Etc.

ARKWRIGHT MILLS,
PATERSON, N. J.

JOHN C. RYLE. 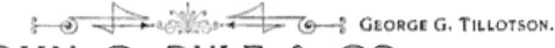 GEORGE G. TILLOTSON.

JOHN C. RYLE & CO.,

Commission Throwsters

OF TRAM, ORGANZINE, ETC.

107 WASHINGTON ST.   PATERSON, N. J.

ESTATE OF GEORGE BARNES,

Oil of Vitriol,
Muriatic Acid,
Aqua Fortis,
Nitric Acid,
Change Acid,
Sulphurous Acid,
Aqua Ammonia,
Glauber Salts,
Sal Soda,
Tin Crystals,
Blue Vitriol,
Copperas, &c.

MANUFACTURING CHEMIST.

Pyroligneous Acid, Acetic Acid

Red Liquor, Iron Liquor, Nitrate of Iron, Bi-Chloride Tin,
Muriates of Iron, Tin, Antimony, &c.

PATERSON, N. J.

HAMIL & BOOTH

Silk Manufacturers,

HAMIL MILL
AND
PASSAIC SILK WORKS.

PATERSON, N. J.

JAMES JACKSON & SONS,

TEXTILE MACHINIST

Jacquard Machines and Compass Boards, Specialties.

VELVETS AND VELVETEENS IN THE GRAY, DYED AND FINISHED.

18 & 20 Albion Avenue, Paterson, N. J.

ADVERTISEMENTS

W. M. INGLIS. A. D. VREELAND.

INGLIS & CO.

Commission SILK THROWSTERS

"GRANT WORKS."

Paterson, N. J.

The Phoenix Silk Manufacturing Co.

PATERSON, N. J.,

—AND—

20-26 GREENE STREET, NEW YORK.

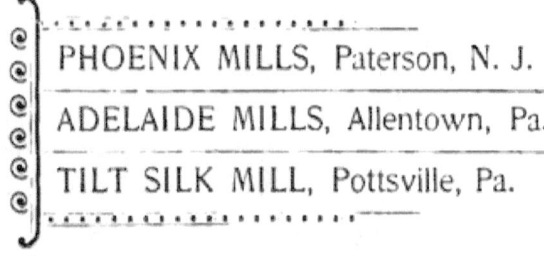

PHOENIX MILLS, Paterson, N. J.

ADELAIDE MILLS, Allentown, Pa.

TILT SILK MILL, Pottsville, Pa.

ALBERT TILT, President.
JOS. W. CONGDON, Vice-President.
JNO. R. CURRAN, Secretary.

COMPLIMENTS OF

JOHNSON, COWDIN & CO.

MANUFACTURERS OF

SILK RIBBONS, * * * *

Riverside, Paterson, N. J.

Manhattan Shirt Mills,

207 to 223 River St.

Our work being steady all the year round, and also of a quality to give satisfaction, thus enabling us to increase our production, we are in a position to give employment to girls on sewing machines, and to young men as ironers, at as good average pay as any mill in town.

CHAS. L. AUGER, Prest. and Treas.   CHARLES SIMON, Sec'y.

The Auger & Simon Silk Dyeing Co.

COLORS AND BLACKS

Paterson, N. J.

Cornforth & Marx,

SILK MANUFACTURERS,

Royle Mill.   PATERSON, N. J.

STANDARD OIL COMPANY,

Paterson Station.

Refiners of Petroleum,

PATERSON, N. J.

S. B. FARNUM, Manager.

KEARNS BROS. Silk Dyers. Specialties: Weighted Blacks and Pure Dye Colors, Organzine and Tram Brights and Heavy Tram Souples, and Fast Blacks and Colors for Velvets, Tailors' Goods, etc. Works: Cor. Wood & Shady sts., Riverside, Paterson, N. J. P. O. Box, No. 665.

LOCKWOOD BROS. & CO.,

FURNITURE, CARPETINGS, OILCLOTHS, REFRIGERATORS, BEDDING,

Draperies and House Furnishing Goods in General.

87 CROSS STREET.   TELEPHONE 223.   290, 292, 294 MAIN ST.

ESTABLISHED 1870.
JOSEPH ATKINSON & SON,
WHOLESALE BAKERS and FLOUR DEALERS

36 HAMBURGH AVENUE,
PATERSON, N. J.

LONG DISTANCE TELEPHONE
—432.—

W. E. KNIPSCHER,
FRANK MAASS.

KNIPSCHER & MAASS

SILK DYERS,

SPECIALTIES,
- HEAVY COLORED SOUPLES
- AND FAST COLORS FOR
- TAILORS' GOODS.
- BLUE BLACKS EQUAL TO
- LYON'S DYE.

VAN HOUTEN
AND MILL STS.,

PATERSON, N. J.

---

30 CENTS A DAY SECURES A HOME,
ON THE INSTALLMENT PLAN IN THREE YEARS.

First-class Building Lots for sale cheap and on easy terms, on Main and adjoining streets. Payment in Installments monthly, according to the price of lots. Ten per cent. will be allowed the purchaser who pays all cash. One payment of $20 on all lots purchased to be paid on the day of sale. A warranty deed will be given to all purchasers, thus guaranteeing the property free from all incumbrances.

JOHN McKIERNAN,
222 MAIN ST.   Of the firm of Doremus & McKiernan.   PATERSON, N. J.

C. W. INGLIS, PRESIDENT.

Paterson Lumber and Wood Working Co.

DOORS, SASH, BLINDS, MOULDINGS, LUMBER, FRAMES, &c.

HARD * WOOD * WORK * A * SPECIALTY.

Railroad Avenue, Slater Street and Dale Avenue,

TELEPHONE 296.   PATERSON, N. J.

1784.   1893.

BARBOUR'S IRISH FLAX

(BARBOUR FLAX SPINNING COMPANY — TRADE MARK — FLAX)

JACQUARD THREAD.

Fine LINEN YARNS for Manufacturing Purposes.

SALESROOMS: No. 218 Church Street,
NEW YORK.

THRIFT & SON,

MANUFACTURERS OF

MOULDINGS,

AND DEALERS IN

SHINGLES, LUMBER, LATH, &c.

424 STRAIGHT ST.,

All kinds of Mill Work to order.   PATERSON, N. J.

JAMES VAN KIRK. A. H. KNAPP.

Midland Coal Yard.

VAN KIRK & KNAPP,

WHOLESALE AND RETAIL DEALERS IN

LEHIGH AND BITUMINOUS COAL.

Yard Cor. Broadway and East 18th St.,

TELEPHONE 221. PATERSON, N. J.

Marshall & Ball,

ONE PRICE

CLOTHIERS,

221 and 223 Main St.,

PATERSON, N., J.

OLDEST HOUSE IN THE BUSINESS.

ESTABLISHED 1828.

THOS. E. O'NEILL,

(Successor to Chas. O'Neill.)

DEALER IN COAL, LUMBER, BLUESTONE AND BUILDING MATERIALS.

STANDARD FOR QUALITY.   230 to 266 Mill Street.

LEHIGH COAL A SPECIALTY. TELEPHONE 191.

Ladders 6c. per foot and upwards.

CORNELIUS WHITE,

LUMBER DEALER

10-20 GOVERNOR STREET,

Telephone 227B.

* * * COMPLIMENTS OF * * *

The Paterson

Brewing Co.

PATERSON, N. J.

Established 1812.
Incorporated 1887.

S. T. Zabriskie, Pres't.   E. Phillips, Sec'y and Treas.

THE ANDERSON LUMBER CO.
DEALERS IN

Lumber, Coal and Masons' Materials,

PACKING CASES, HOUSE, TRIM, SCROLL SAWING AND TURNING.

Mill Yard and Docks Foot of Gregory Ave.,
PASSAIC, N. J.

PATERSON ❋ IRON ❋ CO.

MANUFACTURERS OF Iron & Steel Forgings OF EVERY DESCRIPTION

For Railways, Steamships, Sugar Mills, &c., Forged or Finished.

OFFICE AND WORKS: · PATERSON, N. J.

C. D. BECKWITH, PRESIDENT.

William T. Ryle, Pres.   Arthur Ryle, Treas.   William Strange, Vice-Pres.

Wm. M. Brock, Sec'y and General Manager.

Edison Electric Illuminating Company,

PATERSON, N. J.

INCANDESCENT AND ARC LIGHTING.

——ELECTRIC MOTORS——

Arc Lamps on Low Pressure, *i. e.*, Incandescent Current, a New Feature. Can be turned on and off at all hours by means of a switch, same as Incandescent Lamps.

PRICES FURNISHED UPON APPLICATION.

Chas. O. Brown, Pres't.   G. Planten, Treas.   W. G. A. Miller, Sec'y.

The Riverside Bridge & Iron Works,

ENGINEERS × AND × BRIDGE × BUILDERS,

Railroad Bridges and Heavy Iron Structural Work of Every Description.

WORKS AT   NEW YORK OFFICE,
PATERSON, N. J.   No. 18 BROADWAY.

GAS STOVES FOR HEATING AND COOKING.

WITH THEIR USE **NO** WOOD, COAL, ASHES, DUST, DELAY

The : United : Gas : Improvement : Co.

Gas Office: 146 Ellison Street, Paterson, N. J.

J. S. ROGERS, Pres't.
JOHN HAVRON, Sec'y.
REUBEN WELLS, Supt.
} PATERSON, N. J.

R. S. HUGHES, Treasurer, 44 Exchange Place, NEW YORK.

The ❖ Rogers ❖ Locomotive and ❖ Machine ❖ Works,

OF PATERSON, NEW JERSEY.

NEW YORK OFFICE,
44 EXCHANGE PLACE.

GEO. SWIFT. Established 1844. T. E. SNYDER.

GEO. SWIFT & CO.
Successors to E. B. KING.

Stoves, Ranges and Hot-Air Furnaces,
PLUMBERS, STEAM AND GAS FITTERS.
Tin, Copper and Sheet Iron Workers,
ENGINEERS' SUPPLIES, ETC.
68 AND 70 VAN HOUTEN STREET, PATERSON N. J.

America's Famous Snow Plow

THE ROTARY

The Leslie Bros. Mfg. Co.
PATERSON, N. J.

- Pattern Pine, Pine Lumber,
- Spruce, Hemlock, N. C. Pine,
- Cypress, Yellow Pine,
- White Wood, Ash,
- Oak, Cherry, Walnut.

247 TO 257 MARKET ST.,

200 TO 206 AND 213 TO 217 PATERSON ST.

THE A. HUBBARD LUMBER CO.

- Sash, Doors, Blinds,
- Flooring, Ceiling,
- Sawing, Planing,
- Mouldings, Stairs,
- Millwork of every Description.

OFFICE, No. 247 MARKET ST.,

PATERSON, N. J.

John Royle & Sons,

MACHINISTS

Straight Street, Essex Street and Ramapo Avenue,
NEAR THE ERIE AND THE N. Y., S. & W. R'y Depots.
PATERSON, N. J.

JOHN W. FERGUSON, C. E.
✶ ✶ ENGINEER AND BUILDER ✶ ✶

Contracts taken for all classes of mill and shop construction; complete plans and specifications furnished as part of the contract.
Correspondence is solicited with parties intending to erect buildings of this character, who wish to have the entire work done under one contract, including the engine, boilers, heating apparatus, plumbing, etc.
Satisfactory reference furnished from parties for whom similar work has been done.

OFFICE, PATERSON NATIONAL BANK BUILDING,
PATERSON, N. J.

McNab & Harlin Mfg. Co.

MANUFACTURERS OF

BRASS ✶ COCKS,

PLUMBERS' BRASS WORK,

Globe Valves, Gauge Cocks, Steam Whistles and Water Gauges,

WROUGHT IRON PIPE AND FITTINGS,

PLUMBERS' AND GAS FITTERS' TOOLS,

No. 56 JOHN STREET, NEW YORK.

FACTORY, PATERSON, N. J.

JOHN E. BEGGS, President and Treasurer.

The John E. Beggs Machinery and Supply Co.
P.O. Box 240, Paterson, N. J.
PIPE FITTINGS & VALVES
ENGINES, BOILERS, PUMPS, ETC.
MILL EQUIPMENTS.

74 Cortlandt St.,
New York City.

BRANCH OFFICE
German American Insurance Company,
119 WASHINGTON STREET.
CHAS. REYNOLDS, Manager.

Losses Promptly Settled and Paid at this Office.

Telephone 520.   CALL FOR REFERENCE.

FIRST NATIONAL BANK,
PATERSON, N. J.

United States Depository.

CAPITAL STOCK,	$400,000
SURPLUS AND PROFITS,	320,000
DEPOSITS,	1,800,000

Business and Family Accounts Received.

DIRECTORS.

ALPHEUS S. ALLEN.	JAMES BOOTH.	HENRY B. CROSBY.
GARRET A. HOBART.	W. O. FAYERWEATHER.	JOHN REYNOLDS.
A. W. ROGERS.	GARRET D. VOORHIS.	JOHN J. BROWN.
WM. BARBOUR.	EDWARD T. BELL.	J. W. CLEVELAND.

JOHN J. BROWN, President.
JOHN REYNOLDS, Vice-President.
EDWARD T. BELL, Cashier.
W. G. SCOTT, Assistant Cashier.

OFFICE OF THE
MIESCH MANUFACTURING COMPANY,
LESLIE AND COURTLAND STS.

ADVERTISEMENTS

Paterson Opera House,

JOHN J. GOETSCHENS,
Manager.

Playing only the best Attractions
at Popular Prices.

MATINEES WEDNESDAY AND SATURDAY.

JOHN R. LEE,

Railroad ✦ Contractor,

313 Main Street,

Telephone 360.

Established 1860.   Telephone 133.

J. A. HALL & CO.

MANUFACTURERS OF

Reeds, : Harness, : Lingoes,

MAILS, SHUTTLES,

and General Weavers' Supplies.

Reeds and Harness for Ribbon and
Broad Silk Manufacturers
a specialty.

30 AND 32 HAMILTON AVENUE.

PATERSON, N. J.

HENRY B. KING,

ENGRAVER OF

PRINTERS' ✹ ROLLERS,

Cor. Summer and Fulton Streets.

ADVERTISEMENTS

SECOND NATIONAL BANK,

PATERSON, N. J.

Capital $150,000.   Surplus $100,000.

Established 1864.   Telephone No. 226.

S. S. SHERWOOD,

Real Estate and Insurance Agent

No. 270 MARKET STREET,

Opposite Depots.   PATERSON, N. J.

For many years I have been Selling Well Located Lots on Installments of $5.00 per month under contracts that protect the buyer should he be unable to keep up his payments at any time. During these years there have been no forfeits.

Real Estate Bought, Sold and Exchanged.

MONEY TO LOAN ON BOND AND MORTGAGE,

— AND —

FULL ✦ CHARGE ✦ TAKEN ✦ OF ✦ PROPERTY.

FREDERICK HARDING & SON ••

MANUFACTURERS OF

Paper Boxes.

JACQUARD CARDS A SPECIALTY.   200 and 202 Straight St.

Jos. Heidelberger, Pres't   Wm. M. Smith, Sec'y and Treas.   S. Dringer, Supt.

New Jersey Iron and Metal Company,

—DEALERS IN—

SCRAP IRON, STEEL, COPPER, BRASS, ETC.

OLD BOILERS, ENGINES AND MACHINERY,

Office and Yard, 124 to 130 Railroad Avenue,

PATERSON, N. J.

P. O. Box, 697.   Telephone, 186.

THE MOST COMPLETE PRINTING ESTABLISHMENT IN the EASTERN STATES is at MERIDEN, CONN., and is conducted by : : : : : : : : : : : : :

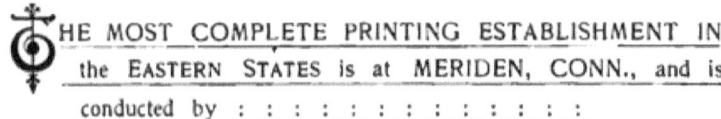

The Journal Publishing Co.

Is it not better to have your WOOD or PHOTO ENGRAVING, ELECTROTYPING, PRINTING and BINDING done under one roof than by as many separate parties? And then, too, why pay four profits when we combine the work and are satisfied with one?

Let us estimate for you and tell your friends about us.

We are Manufacturers of
     LEATHER CASES,
     PORTFOLIOS and
     SPECIALLY RULED and
     PRINTED ACCOUNT BOOKS,

And the Only Manufacturers in the State of

SILK BADGES, STAMPED IN GOLD, SILVER OR INK, for Clubs, Societies, Reunions and Conventions.

The Hartford Times on Dec. 3, 1892, says editorially :

Throughout this State the largest circulation is in nearly every instance enjoyed by one or the other of the evening papers in each community, notably so in the case of   *   *   *   *   THE JOURNAL, in Meriden, etc.

Send us your address for advertising rates and sample copies. Address,

The Journal Publishing Co.

MERIDEN, CONN.

The Paterson Safe Deposit and Trust Co.

NO. 152 MARKET STREET,
Opposite New City Hall.

BANKING DEPARTMENT,

Accounts opened for $1 or any larger sum. Interest allowed on deposits.

SAFE DEPOSIT DEPARTMENT,

Small Safes and Boxes rented in fire and burglar proof vaults at a nominal yearly rental.

JOHN W. GRIGGS, President.
JAMES INGLIS, JR., Vice-President.
F. R. ALLEN, Treas.

THE PATERSON NATIONAL BANK.

STATE, CITY AND COUNTY DEPOSITORY.
Began Business July 10, 1889.

CAPITAL,	$300,000
SURPLUS AND PROFITS,	75,000
DEPOSITS,	1,200,000

WILLIAM STRANGE, President.
HARWOOD B. PARKE, Vice-President.
HENRY C. KNOX, Cashier.

DIRECTORS.

WATTS COOKE.   HON. JOHN W. GRIGGS.   JOHN S. COOKE.
WILLIAM BARBOUR.   FRANK W. ALLEN.   SAMUEL J. WATSON.
BERNARD KATZ.   WILLIAM STRANGE.   WILLIAM T. RYLE.
SAMUEL V. S. MUZZY.   HENRY C. KNOX.
HARWOOD B. PARKE.

BUSINESS AND PERSONAL ACCOUNTS INVITED.

www.ingramcontent.com/pod-product-compliance
Lightning Source LLC
Chambersburg PA
CBHW022014220426
43663CB00007B/1079